BY THE EDITORS OF CONSUMER GUIDE®

FAVORITE BRAND NAME RECIPES

Desserts for All Occasions

Contents

1985 edition published by Beekman House
Distributed by Crown Publishers, Inc.
225 Park Avenue South
New York, New York 10003

Manufactured in the United States of America
h g f e d c b a

ISBN 0-517-60406-X

Front Cover
Top row from left:
Mocha Mousse (Hiram Walker Inc.)
Magic Cookie Bars (Borden Inc.)
Bottom row from left:
Chocolate Peanut Ripple Cake (The Pillsbury Co.)
Eggnog Custard Pie (Michigan Fruit Canners)
Back Cover
Top row from left:
Peach Melba Cake (Thomas J. Lipton, Inc.)
Bits 'O Brickle® Ice Cream Pie & Sauce (L. S. Heath &
    Sons, Inc.)
Bottom row from left:
Sunlite® Carrot Cake (Hunt-Wesson Kitchens)
Choco-Bar Fondue (Hershey Foods Corp.)

Cover Design: Phyllis Ritthaler

Introduction

This book truly has wonderful, luscious recipes to impress your guests, such as, ''Fluted Chocolate Cups'' filled with scrumptious ''Chocolate Mousse,'' or the lovely ''Miniature Baked Alaskas.'' Serve any of our fruit desserts after a large meal, such as ''Poached Pears With Raspberry Sauce'' or the elegant ''Coupes Napoleon.'' Try the quick and easy ''Fruit Tostadas'' or ''Tacos'' for a surprise delight. We have chocolate cakes, chiffon cakes, pudding cakes, strawberry shortcakes and cheesecakes galore. Simple coffee cakes and the always popular ''Pineapple Pecan Rolls'' too. Pie recipes that include fruit pies, cream and chiffon pies, ice cream pies, custard, pumpkin and mince pies, and, of course, brownies, cookies and candies for the holidays. There are also Low Calorie and Low Cholesterol recipes included to help the diet watchers.

All of us made this recipe collection possible by taking certain recipes that first appeared on food product labels or in advertisements and choosing them as our favorites! We have included only quality recipes that are or will soon become family treasures. The recipes are reprinted exactly as they appear on the labels or in the advertisements.

For the convenience of our readers we have included an address directory of all food manufacturers listed in the book (see **ACKNOWLEDGMENTS**). Any questions or comments should be directed to the individual manufacturers for prompt attention. All recipes in this book have been copyrighted by the food manufacturers and cannot be reprinted without their permission. By printing these recipes, CONSUMER GUIDE® is *not* endorsing particular brand name foods.

Prepare any dessert from this wonderful book today and be prepared for compliments tonight!

Ambrosia Crepes

2 cans (13½ oz. each) pineapple tidbits, well drained
3 cups halved orange sections *OR* drained Mandarin orange segments
1 cup flaked coconut
1 cup dairy sour cream
20 crepes*

Combine all ingredients except crepes. Chill to blend flavors while preparing crepes. Spread scant ⅓ cup filling on each crepe and roll up. *Makes approx. 6 cups filling*

*Basic Crepe Recipe

6 tablespoons butter
6 eggs, slightly beaten
1 cup milk
1 cup water
1½ cups all-purpose flour
½ teaspoon salt

Melt butter in 10-inch omelet pan or 8-inch crepe pan. In bowl beat eggs, milk, water and melted butter (Set aside skillet.) together with rotary beater. Blend in flour and salt until mixture is smooth. On medium-high heat, heat buttered omelet pan until just hot enough to sizzle a drop of water. For each crepe pour scant ¼ cup batter in pan, rotating pan as batter is poured. Cook until lightly browned on bottom; remove from pan or, if desired, turn and brown other side.* Stack between sheets of paper toweling or waxed paper until ready to use. (Crepes may be frozen.) Spread scant ⅓ cup filling on each crepe; roll up. Serve 2-3 crepes per person. *Makes approx. 20 crepes*

*Crepes to be filled need only be browned on one side. Use unbrowned side for filling.

Note: Crepes should set to a thin lacy pancake almost immediately. If too much batter is poured into pan, pour off excess immediately. If there are holes, add a drop or two of batter for a patch.

Favorite recipe from the **American Egg Board**

Choco-Bar Fondue

2 HERSHEY'S® Milk Chocolate Bars (8 ounces)
1 HERSHEY'S® Semi-Sweet Chocolate Bar (4 ounces)
¾ cup light cream
2 to 3 tablespoons kirsch, orange-flavored liqueur, or ½ teaspoon almond extract (optional)
Fondue Dippers*

Combine chocolate bars and cream in a heavy saucepan; stir constantly over medium-low heat until chocolate is melted. Just before serving, add liqueur or almond extract; pour into fondue pot or chafing dish. Serve warm with a selection of fondue dippers. *About 2½ cups fondue*

*Fondue Dippers

Fruits:
1. Strawberries
2. Pineapple chunks
3. Grapes
4. Cherries
5. Mandarine or fresh orange segments
6. Apple slices*
7. Pear slices
8. Peach slices
9. Banana slices*

Other Treats:
1. Marshmallows
2. Ladyfingers
3. Bite-size pieces of angel food or pound cake
4. Miniature cream puffs
5. Nuts
6. Pretzels
7. Cookies

*Brush slices with lemon juice to prevent browning.

Soufflé Normande

3 cups sliced pared apples
1 tablespoon lemon juice
⅓ cup **BLUE BONNET® Margarine**
½ cup sugar
¼ cup **LEMON HART Golden Jamaica Rum**

Soufflé Mixture:

5 eggs, separated (at room temperature)
½ cup sugar
3 tablespoons **BLUE BONNET® Margarine**, melted
3 tablespoons flour
¼ teaspoon salt
1 cup milk
1 teaspoon vanilla extract

Sprinkle apple slices with lemon juice. In large skillet melt ⅓ cup **BLUE BONNET® Margarine**. Sauté apples in margarine until tender, about 8 minutes. Pour ½ cup sugar over apples, and stir gently for a few minutes, until the sugar caramelizes. Pour **LEMON HART Rum** over apples, set aflame, and shake the pan until the flame goes out. Set aside.

SOUFFLÉ MIXTURE:
In small deep bowl, beat egg yolks until thick and lemon colored. Gradually beat in ¼ cup sugar. Combine 3 tablespoons melted **BLUE BONNET® Margarine**, flour and salt in heavy saucepan. Gradually add milk. Cook over low heat, stirring constantly, until smooth and thick, about 5 minutes. Slowly beat hot mixture into beaten egg yolks. Stir in vanilla extract. Cool slightly. Beat egg whites until frothy; slowly beat in remaining ¼ cup of sugar and continue to beat to make stiff meringue. Fold a quarter of the egg whites into the egg yolk mixture; then fold all back lightly and evenly into the remaining egg whites.

Place sautéed apples in bottom of 2-quart soufflé dish; top with soufflé mixture. With spatula, make a slight indentation around top of soufflé, 1-inch from edge. Bake at 350°F. for about 35 to 40 minutes, or until fairly firm. Serve immediately.

Makes 6 to 8 servings

KNOX®

Black Forest Soufflé

1 can (16 oz.) sour pitted cherries, drained
5 tablespoons cherry brandy or brandy
4 squares (1 oz. ea.) semi-sweet chocolate
2 envelopes **KNOX® Unflavored Gelatine**
¾ cup sugar
3 eggs, separated
2 cups milk
1½ teaspoons vanilla extract
2 cups (1 pt.) whipping or heavy cream

Reserve ½ cup cherries. Chop remaining cherries and marinate in 2 tablespoons brandy. Make enough chocolate curls for garnish (about ¼ oz. chocolate); reserve.

In medium saucepan, mix unflavored gelatine with ½ cup sugar; blend in egg yolks beaten with milk. Let stand 1 minute. Stir over low heat until gelatine is completely dissolved, about 5 minutes. Add remaining chocolate (about 3¾ oz.) and continue cooking, stirring constantly, until chocolate is melted. With wire whip or rotary beater, beat mixture until chocolate is blended. Stir in remaining brandy and vanilla. Pour into large bowl and chill, stirring occasionally, until mixture mounds slightly when dropped from spoon.

In large bowl, beat egg whites until soft peaks form; gradually add remaining sugar and beat until stiff. Fold into gelatine mixture. In medium bowl, whip 1½ cups cream; fold into gelatine mixture with chopped cherries and brandy. Turn into 1-quart soufflé dish with 3-inch collar; chill until set. Remove collar; garnish with remaining cream, whipped, reserved cherries and chocolate curls.

Makes about 10 servings

Gerber®

Walnut Prune Soufflé

4 egg whites
⅛ teaspoon cream of tartar
¼ teaspoon salt
¼ cup sugar
2 jars (4¾ oz. each) **GERBER® Strained Prunes**
½ teaspoon vanilla
½ teaspoon cinnamon
⅔ cup walnuts, chopped

Beat egg whites until foamy, add cream of tartar and salt, and continue beating to form soft peaks. Gradually add sugar beating until stiff peaks form. Gently fold in prunes, vanilla, cinnamon and walnuts. Turn into a buttered 1½ quart soufflé dish. Set dish in pan of warm water and bake in preheated 325°F. oven for 40-50 minutes or until firm. Garnish with sweetened whipped cream. Serve at once.

Royal®

Chocolate Pecan Puff

1 package (regular size) **ROYAL® Chocolate Pudding**
1 tablespoon sugar
2 cups milk
1 package (3-ounce) **ROYAL® Cherry Gelatin**
1 cup boiling water
½ cup cold water
1 cup heavy cream, whipped
½ cup finely chopped **PLANTERS® or SOUTHERN BELLE Pecans**

Empty **ROYAL® Chocolate Pudding** into saucepan. Add sugar; gradually blend in milk, stirring to keep mixture smooth. Cook over medium high heat, stirring steadily, until mixture just starts to boil. Place wax paper or plastic wrap directly on pudding; chill at least 1 hour. Dissolve **ROYAL® Cherry Gelatin** in boiling water. Add cold water. Chill until slightly thickened. Fold in cooled pudding, whipped cream and **PLANTERS® or SOUTHERN BELLE Pecans**. Pour into 6-cup mold. Chill until firm. Unmold; if desired, garnish with additional whipped cream.

Makes 6 to 8 servings

Dubonnet Tortoni

¾ cup sugar
¼ cup water
5 egg yolks, beaten
⅜ cup **DUBONNET Rouge** aperitif wine
2 cups heavy cream, whipped

In saucepan combine sugar and water. Bring to a boil and boil for 5 minutes. Stir into egg yolks and stir over hot, but not boiling water, until custard is thick. Cool. Stir in **DUBONNET Rouge** and fold in heavy cream. Freeze in home freezer.

Makes 5 cups

Strawberry Cream Charlotte

3 pints fresh California strawberries, washed and
   stemmed
1 tablespoon lime or lemon juice
2 envelopes unflavored gelatine
½ cup sugar
4 eggs, separated
1¼ cups milk*
4 ounces semisweet chocolate, melted
12 ladyfingers, split
1 cup **BLUE RIBBON®** Sliced Natural Almonds,
   toasted
1 cup (½ pint) whipping or heavy cream, whipped
Whipped cream (recipe follows)

Slice enough strawberries to equal 5 cups; reserve remaining strawberries for garnish. In blender or food processor, puree 3 cups sliced strawberries. Combine with lime juice; set aside. In medium saucepan, mix unflavored gelatine with ¼ cup sugar; blend in egg yolks beaten with milk. Let stand 1 minute. Stir over low heat until gelatine is completely dissolved, about 5 minutes; stir in pureed strawberries. Pour into large bowl and chill, stirring occasionally, until mixture mounds slightly when dropped from spoon.

Meanwhile, prepare pan; spread melted chocolate over rounded sides of ladyfingers. Sprinkle with almonds, pressing gently to coat. Stand ladyfingers, coated side out, against sides of 9-inch springform pan. In large bowl, beat egg whites until soft peaks form; gradually add remaining sugar and beat until stiff. Fold egg whites, then whipped cream and remaining 2 cups sliced strawberries into gelatine mixture. Turn into prepared pan; chill until firm. Garnish with reserved strawberries, halved, and whipped cream.

Makes about 12 servings

*VARIATION:
Substitute ¼ cup almond-flavored liqueur for ¼ cup milk.

Chef's Secret Whipped Cream

Unflavored gelatine is the ''secret'' to fluffy whipped cream that won't wilt so quickly when used as a topping for strawberry shortcakes or other desserts. In small saucepan, mix ½ teaspoon unflavored gelatine with 1 tablespoon cold water. Let stand 1 minute. Stir over medium heat until gelatine is completely dissolved, about 1 minute. Pour into small bowl. Quickly stir in 1 cup heavy or whipping cream and beat until stiff; chill.

IMPERIAL **Pure Cane** SUGAR®

Poteet Strawberry Pyramid

1 cup **IMPERIAL Granulated Sugar**
1 cup heavy cream
2 cups sour cream
Shiny decorative fresh leaves
1 pint whole strawberries (fresh or frozen)
Raspberries, (fresh or frozen)
IMPERIAL 10X Powdered Sugar

Combine **IMPERIAL Granulated Sugar** and heavy cream; gently combine this mixture with sour cream. Chill until thickened. Arrange decorative leaves in circle on serving plate. Put about ½ cup of cream in center and begin arranging strawberries around edges and in center of cream. Add more cream and more strawberries on top of first layer and continue to build into tapering tower. When ready to serve, drizzle mashed, sweetened raspberries over top of chilled strawberry pyramid. Dust with **IMPERIAL 10X Powdered Sugar**.

Serves 6 to 8

Dorman's® Muenster Dessert Quiche

8-10 slices white bread, crusts removed
½ cup apricot jam
2 cups milk
½ cup wheat germ
¼ cup firmly packed light brown sugar
6 slices **DORMAN'S® Muenster Cheese**, grated in
   blender
4 eggs
½ teaspoon salt
Whipped cream, optional

Fit 2 slices bread and 4 triangular shaped half slices of bread onto the bottom of a greased 8-inch spring form pan. Use small pieces of bread to cover bottom completely. Cut remaining bread slices in half. Place around edge of pan to form side crust. Press with finger tips firmly and evenly. Spread jam evenly over inside of crust. Combine remaining ingredients until well blended. Pour into crust. Bake at 375°F. for 20 minutes or until lightly browned. Cool. Gently remove side of pan. If desired, serve with whipped cream.

Makes 6-8 servings

Peppermint Rice Cloud

1 bag **SUCCESS® Rice**
1 cup milk
1½ cups miniature marshmallows
⅓ cup crushed peppermint candy
½ cup heavy cream
1 tablespoon sugar
1 teaspoon vanilla
Chocolate sauce

Cook bag of rice according to package directions. Drain bag and pour out water.

In same saucepan, empty the rice and add the milk, marshmallows, and candy. Cook and stir over medium heat for 5 minutes, or until marshmallows and candy melt. Remove from heat and cool.

Whip cream, gradually adding sugar and vanilla. Beat until stiff peaks form.

Fold whipped cream into cooled rice mixture. Pour into serving dish and chill. Garnish with Chocolate sauce, if desired.

Makes 6 servings (about ½ cup each)

Italian Delight

1 3-ounce package lady fingers
¼ cup **HOLLAND HOUSE® Marsala Cooking Wine**
2 eggs, separated
½ cup granulated sugar
1 cup ricotta or cream cheese
5 ounces chocolate bits
30 macaroons, crushed

Sprinkle lady fingers with Marsala. In a mixing bowl, beat egg yolks with sugar and cheese until ingredients thicken. In a separate bowl, beat egg whites with an electric beater or whisk until stiff. Fold the chocolate bits and macaroons into the egg whites. Line a 1-quart glass bowl with the lady fingers. Fold egg yolk and egg white mixtures together and place in mold. Freeze overnight. Unmold and serve.   *Serves 6*

Fresh Yogurt Sundae

1 cup **DANNON® Plain Yogurt**
2 Tbsp. honey
2 Tbsp. chopped almonds
Chopped dates

Put yogurt into chilled sherbet cup. Pour honey over yogurt, sprinkle with almonds and dates.   *Makes 1 serving*

Strawberry Ribbon Loaf

2 (3 ounce) packages strawberry gelatin
1 jar (15 ounce) applesauce
18 double **SUNSHINE® Honey Graham Crackers**
1 envelope **DREAM WHIP® Whipped Topping Mix**
3 tablespoons confectioners' sugar
1 cup fresh strawberries

Combine gelatin and applesauce in a small mixing bowl, stirring until well blended. Place 2 double crackers end to end, on a platter; spread with ¼ cup applesauce mixture. Repeat layers, ending with crackers. Prepare whipped topping as directed on package, adding confectioners' sugar before beating; spread over top and sides of loaf. Chill 30 minutes. Garnish with strawberry halves.   *Yield: 10 servings*

Lemon Refrigerator Dessert

22 gingersnaps or graham crackers
¼ cup butter (or margerine)
1 can **LUCKY LEAF® Lemon Pie Filling**
¾ cup water
½ cup evaporated milk, chilled
1 Tbsp. lemon juice

Crush gingersnaps or graham crackers and mix with softened butter. Spread ½ crumbs in 9″ square baking pan. Mix pie filling with water until well blended. Whip evaporated milk until fluffy. Add lemon juice. Continue beating until stiff. Fold into lemon mixture. Pour over crumbs in pan. Top with remaining crumbs. Chill in freezer compartment at least 1 hour.

Scrumptious Dessert

¼ lb. margarine or butter
2 tablespoons sugar
1 cup flour
1 (8 oz.) package cream cheese
⅔ cup powdered sugar
2 (8 oz.) cartons of whipped topping
1 can **THANK YOU® BRAND Chocolate Pudding**
1 can **THANK YOU® BRAND Vanilla Pudding**

1. Cream margarine and sugar, add flour, mix well. Bake in 9 × 13 × 2 inch baking pan in 350° oven. Cool.
2. Mix cream cheese, sugar, and one carton of whipped topping until creamy. Spread on baked crust.
3. Mix chocolate and vanilla pudding. Spread over cheese mixture. Spread remaining whipped topping over top. Chill.

Light-as-Mist Apple Cream

1 envelope unflavored gelatin
¼ cup cold water
1½ cups light cream
½ cup sugar
⅛ teaspoon salt
1 cup sour cream
1 cup applesauce
¼ cup **JOHNNIE WALKER RED** Scotch

Soften gelatin in cold water in small saucepan. Stir in light cream, sugar and salt. Cook, stirring, over low heat until gelatin and sugar dissolve. Remove from heat; beat in sour cream until smooth. Stir in applesauce and **JOHNNIE WALKER RED**. Pour into 4 serving dishes. Garnish as desired. Chill until set.

Pacific Ginger Torte

1 can (1 lb., 4 oz.) **DOLE® Crushed Pineapple**
1 package (14.5 oz.) gingerbread mix
½ cup dairy sour cream
1 large banana, sliced
2 tablespoons lemon juice
½ pint whipping cream
1 teaspoon vanilla
¼ cup powdered sugar
½ cup chopped walnuts

Drain pineapple reserving ½ cup syrup. Blend reserved pineapple syrup into gingerbread mix. Beat in sour cream. Pour into two greased 8-inch round cake pans. Bake in a preheated oven 350° F. 20 to 25 minutes until it tests done. Turn out onto wire racks to cool. Meanwhile slice banana into lemon juice and toss to coat each slice well. Whip cream with vanilla and sugar until stiff. Place one layer gingerbread on serving plate. Spread with half whipped cream. Arrange banana slices around edge. Spoon half of drained pineapple into center. Top with remaining gingerbread layer. Spread with remaining whipped cream. Ring edge with walnuts, spoon remaining pineapple into center.

Makes 8 to 10 servings

"Carnival" Apricot-Date Torte

1 (17 oz.) can **S&W® Peeled Apricots**, drained and cut in quarters
1 cup **S&W® Apricot Nectar**
⅔ cup chopped **S&W® Pitted Dates**
½ cup brown sugar
1 Tbsp. cornstarch
1 Tbsp. lemon juice
1 cup all-purpose flour
1 tsp. baking powder
¼ tsp. salt
½ cup butter or margarine
½ cup sugar
3 egg yolks
1 tsp. vanilla
½ cup chopped **S&W® Pecans**

Meringue:
3 egg whites
¼ tsp. cream of tartar
1 cup brown sugar
1 tsp. vanilla
½ cup chopped **S&W® Pecans**

In saucepan combine apricots, apricot nectar, dates, brown sugar and cornstarch. Cook over medium heat until slightly thickened. Add lemon juice and cool. Sift together flour, baking powder and salt. Cream butter and sugar. Add egg yolks and vanilla. Beat well. Add dry ingredients and pecans and spread in a 12 × 8 well-greased pan. Pour cooled apricot-date mixture over dough. Beat egg whites and cream of tartar until soft mounds form. Gradually add sugar and beat until stiff. Fold in vanilla and pecans. Cover filling with meringue. Bake at 300° for 50 to 60 minutes.

Marita's Linzertorte

1¾ cups **CERESOTA** or **HECKER'S Unbleached Flour**, sifted
½ teaspoon baking powder
½ cup sugar
¼ teaspoon (⅛ if salted butter is used) salt
½ teaspoon cinnamon
Dash (less than ⅛ teaspoon) cloves
1½ cups raw filbert nuts, finely ground and measured after grinding
1 egg, separated
1¼ sticks butter (or margarine)
5-6 tablespoons raspberry jam
1 teaspoon milk

Sift flour, baking powder, sugar, salt and spices into a large bowl. Mix in the nuts. Add the white of egg and half the yolk (reserve remaining half), and mix. Cut in butter until the mixture resembles a coarse meal.

Working the dough with your hands, press it into a ball. (If it gets sticky, put it in the refrigerator for a little while.) Take about ¾ of the dough and, again with your hands, press it into a 9″ pie

pan, working it up the sides like a pie shell. Spread jam over the center, and not quite to the edges.

On a lightly floured board, press out the remaining piece of dough with your hands to about ¼″ thickness. (It's easier to work this with your hands than with a rolling pin because it's a very crumbly dough.)

Cut out strips about ¾″ wide and criss-cross them lattice fashion over the jam. Make one thin rope out of the remaining strips and circle the top edge with it. Score with a spoon handle, press it with your thumbprint, or decorate it however you'd like.

Mix the remaining half egg yolk with milk, and brush it on the pastry.

Bake in a preheated 350° oven for about 35 mintues, or until browned.

Apricot Linzer Torte

1 cup butter
¼ tsp. salt
2 cups sifted flour
1 cup ground blanched almonds
½ tsp. cinnamon
¼ tsp. allspice
1 tsp. cocoa
Juice and grated rind of ½ lemon
1 heaping cup confectioner's sugar
1 to 1½ cups **SIMON FISCHER Apricot Butter**

Mix all ingredients except Apricot Butter in electric mixer. When thoroughly mixed, knead until smooth; chill. Roll two-thirds of the dough ¼″ thick and line either a torte pan or an 8″ spring form pan, forming a good edge with the dough. Spread generously with Apricot Butter. Roll remaining dough into strips ¼″ wide and place criss-cross over Apricot Butter, making a lattice topping. Place 1 wide strip around cake edge to hold filling secure. Brush dough with slightly beaten egg white. Bake in moderate oven, 350 degrees, 45 to 55 minutes. When cool, fill squares formed by lattice topping with more Apricot Butter so it looks plump and fat, sprinkle with additional powdered sugar. Serve warm or cold.

Chocolate Mousse
(Low Calorie/Low Fat)

1 envelope unflavored gelatin
2 tablespoons unsweetened cocoa
2 eggs, separated
2 cups low-fat milk, divided
5 packets **SWEET 'N LOW®**
1½ teaspoons vanilla

In medium-size saucepan, mix gelatin and cocoa. In separate bowl, beat egg yolks with 1 cup milk. Blend into gelatin mixture. Let stand 1 minute to soften gelatin. Stir over low heat until gelatin is completely dissolved, about 5 minutes. Add remaining milk, **SWEET 'N LOW®**, and vanilla. Pour into large bowl and chill, stirring occasionally, until mixture mounds slightly when dropped from spoon. In separate large bowl, beat egg whites until soft peaks form; gradually add gelatin mixture and beat until doubled in volume, about 5 minutes. Chill until mixture is slightly thickened. Turn into dessert dishes or 1-quart bowl and chill until set.

8 servings

Per Serving (½ cup): Calories: 65; Fat: 3g

Turkey Torte

Pour ½ cup **WILD TURKEY LIQUEUR®** into 8-inch pie plate or saucer. Dip 14 full-size graham crackers in liqueur. Spread ¾ cup apricot preserves on top of 13 crackers. Place on top of each other. Omit preserves from top cracker. In medium saucepan melt 1 package (12 oz.) semisweet chocolate bits with 1 can (14 oz.) sweetened condensed milk. Stir in 1 Tbsp. instant coffee. Cool. Spread top and sides of graham layers. Garnish with almonds. Chill several hours or overnight.

Low Sodium Chocolate Mousse

1 pkg. (12 oz.) semi-sweet chocolate pieces
½ cup boiling water
2 teaspoons **ANGOSTURA®** Aromatic Bitters
4 egg yolks
4 egg whites, stiffly beaten

In a blender, combine chocolate pieces, boiling water, **ANGOSTURA®** and egg yolks. Whirl until smooth and cool to room temperature. Beat egg whites in a bowl until stiff. Fold in chocolate mixture. Spoon mixture into serving dishes. Chill for several hours. Serve with demi-tasse. *Serves 6*

Per serving: Sodium 37 mg; Calories 325

Bénédictine Mousse

6 egg yolks, room temperature
¾ cup **BÉNÉDICTINE** Liqueur
2 cups heavy cream
Pecan halves for garnish

Place egg yolks in the container of a blender; process at low speed. In a small saucepan, heat **BÉNÉDICTINE** until it comes to a full rolling boil. Pour hot liqueur in a steady stream into the egg yolks, with the blender motor running. Process until the mixture becomes a thick custard. Chill. Beat heavy cream until stiff. Remove 1 cup. Fold chilled **BÉNÉDICTINE** mixture into whipped cream. Pour into 8 serving dishes. Garnish with reserved whipped cream and pecan halves. *Serves 8*

KNOX®
Twenty-Minute Mousse

2 envelopes **KNOX®** Unflavored Gelatine
½ cup cold water
1 cup boiling water
2 cups (1 pt.) sherbet, any flavor
1 container (9 oz.) frozen whipped topping, thawed

In large bowl, sprinkle unflavored gelatine over cold water; let stand 1 minute. Add boiling water and stir until gelatine is completely dissolved. With wire whip or rotary beater, blend in sherbet until melted, then whipped topping. Spoon into dessert dishes; chill 15 minutes. *Makes about 8 servings*

Ghirardelli® Chocolate Mousse

1 bar (4 oz.) **GHIRARDELLI®** Semi-Sweet Chocolate
2 Tbsp. water
2 eggs, separated
Pinch salt
⅓ cup sugar
¾ cup whipping cream

In heavy saucepan on low heat, melt broken chocolate with water, stirring constantly. Beat egg yolks until thick. Stirring quickly, add yolks to chocolate; remove from heat. Beat egg whites with salt, gradually adding sugar and beating until stiff peaks form. Fold chocolate into whites. Whip cream and fold into chocolate mixture. Pour into small stemmed glasses. Chill several hours or overnight. Each serving may be topped with whipped cream and chocolate curls, if desired. *Makes 6 (½ cup) servings*

Tia Maria
Frozen Tia Maria® Mousse Cake

Crust:
3 cups (12 ounces) chocolate wafer crumbs
1 stick (½ cup) plus 2 tablespoons butter, melted

Mousse:
8 ounces semisweet chocolate broken into pieces
¼ cup boiling water
½ cup sugar, divided
4 egg yolks, extra large
½ cup **TIA MARIA®** liqueur
4 egg whites, extra large
¼ teaspoon cream of tartar
2 cups heavy cream

Additional **TIA MARIA®** for sauce

CRUST:
Preheat the oven to 375°F. Lightly butter the sides of a 9 × 3-inch spring form pan. Mix the wafer crumbs and melted butter. Press the mixture firmly against the bottom and sides of the pan. Bake for 8 minutes. Let cool.

MOUSSE:
Melt chocolate pieces with ¼ cup sugar and the boiling water in the top of a double boiler. Remove from heat, beat in egg yolks. Return and cook over hot water for 1 minute. Add **TIA MARIA®**, blend thoroughly and set aside to cool completely. Beat egg whites with cream of tartar until stiff; add remaining ¼ cup sugar gradually and beat until stiff peaks form. Fold into chocolate gradually. Whip cream and fold into the mixture; blend well.

ASSEMBLY:
Set a small shot glass in the center of the baked springform pan.* Spoon in the mousse mixture around the glass and fill the shell. Smooth out the top, cover with plastic wrap and freeze several hours or overnight. Decorate the cake with chocolate shavings, if desired. Or if time permits, make attractice chocolate leaves by painting the underside of fresh leaves (ivy or rose are good

choices) with melted semisweet chocolate. Place leaves on saucer and freeze. When ready to serve, remove the springform sides from the cake. Slide onto a serving plate. Peel away the green leaves from the chocolate and arrange on top of cake. Fill the center shot glass with **TIA MARIA®** and serve as a sauce for each piece of cake.

Serves 10 to 12

*If desired, a chocolate cup can be made or purchased to replace shot glass.

Nestlé

Super Chocolate Mousse

One 12-oz. pkg. (2 cups) **NESTLÉ Semi-Sweet Real Chocolate Morsels**
1 cup sugar, divided
¼ cup water
¼ cup brandy
4 egg yolks, beaten
1½ cups heavy cream
1 measuring tablespoon vanilla extract
6 egg whites

Garnish (optional):
Whipped cream

In large heavy gauge saucepan, combine **NESTLÉ Semi-Sweet Real Chocolate Morsels**, ½ cup sugar, water and brandy. Cook over low heat until morsels melt and mixture is smooth; stirring constantly. Bring *just to a boil* over low heat; stirring occasionally. Remove from heat; set aside. In large bowl, gradually beat melted chocolate mixture into beaten egg yolks, using a wire whisk. Beat until smooth. Chill chocolate mixture over ice bath for about 10 minutes or until mixture mounds from spoon; stirring occasionally.* In small chilled bowl, beat heavy cream and vanilla extract until stiff peaks form; set aside. In large bowl, beat egg whites until soft peaks form. Gradually add remaining ½ cup sugar, beating until stiff peaks form. Gradually fold a small amount of beaten egg whites into chilled chocolate mixture. Then fold in remaining egg whites. Fold in whipped cream. Pour into 8-cup soufflé dish. Chill in refrigerator several hours. Garnish with rosettes of whipped cream piped through decorative tube, if desired. Refrigerate until ready to serve.

Makes: about 15-16 servings

*Chocolate mixture sets up quickly. It is necessary to see that chocolate does not solidify on the bottom and sides of bowl.

Domino®

Frozen Peach Mousse

1 cup mashed fresh peaches (or canned, frozen)
¼ teaspoon mace
1 teaspoon grated lemon rind
1 cup heavy cream, whipped
2 egg whites
¼ teaspoon salt
⅓ cup **DOMINO® Golden Light Brown Sugar**, firmly packed

Fold peaches, mace, and lemon rind into whipped cream. Beat egg whites with salt and sugar until stiff. Fold into creamed mixture. Pour mousse into ice cube tray; freeze at lowest temperature until firm. About 1½ hours.

Makes 5 to 6 servings

DANNON® YOGURT

Boysenberry Mousse

2 envelopes **KNOX® Unflavored Gelatine**
½ cup sugar, divided
⅛ teaspoon salt
3 eggs, separated
1 cup milk
2 cups **DANNON® Boysenberry Yogurt**
1 cup heavy cream

Combine gelatine, ¼ cup sugar and salt in medium saucepan. Mix together yolks and milk in medium bowl and stir into gelatine. Place over low heat; stir constantly until gelatine dissolves, about 6 minutes. Cool slightly and add yogurt. Chill, stirring occasionally, until mixture mounds slightly when dropped from a spoon. Beat egg whites until soft peaks form, beat in remaining ¼ cup sugar and beat until stiff. Whip heavy cream until still. Fold egg whites and whipped cream into boysenberry mixture. Turn into 9-cup mold and chill several hours or overnight.

Yield: 10 servings

Fluted Chocolate Cups

1½ cups **HERSHEY'S® Semi-Sweet Chocolate Mini Chips**
Mini Chip Marshmallow Mousse*

Partially melt chocolate Mini Chips in top of double boiler, set over hot, not boiling, water or in microwave. When chocolate is half melted, remove from heat and let stand to melt completely. Place twelve 2¾-inch paper baking cups in muffin pan. Thickly and evenly coat the inside pleated surface and bottom with chocolate using a small dry pastry brush. Chill 10 minutes, coat any thin spots. Chill overnight.

Remove only a few chocolate cups from refrigerator at a time; gently peel paper baking cups from chocolate. (Cups keep weeks if stored in air-tight container in refrigerator.) Several hours before serving, fill with Mini Chip Marshmallow Mousse. Chill or freeze. Garnish with sweetened whipped cream and fresh fruit, if desired.

12 servings

Mini Chip Marshmallow Mousse

1½ cups miniature marshmallows
⅓ cup milk
1 cup **HERSHEY'S® Semi-Sweet Chocolate Mini Chips**
1 cup heavy cream

Combine marshmallows and milk in saucepan; stir over very low heat until marshmallows are melted. Remove from heat; immediately add **Mini Chips**. Stir until melted; cool completely. Whip cream until stiff; fold into chocolate mixture. Spoon into chocolate cups.

MINT VARIATION:

Add ½ teaspoon peppermint extract and garnish with mint leaves.

9

DuBouchett Mocha Mousse

8 Tbsp. liqueur—half **DuBOUCHETT Dark Creme de Cacoa**, half **DuBOUCHETT Coffee Brandy**
2 Tbsp. water
2/3 cup sugar
Pinch of salt
1 egg, beaten
2 Tbsp. sifted confectioners sugar
1 pint heavy cream, stiffly whipped

Cook 6 Tbsp. of the liqueur with next 3 ingredients until syrup will spin a thread (230°). Slowly add syrup and remaining liqueur to beaten egg, beating constantly. Cook in double boiler, stirring constantly, about 5 minutes, or until thickened. Cool mixture, then refrigerate until cold. Blend well, and fold liqueur mixture and sugar into whipped cream. Put mixture in fancy 1 qt. mold and freeze.
Serves 4

Mocha Mousse

1½ cups milk
1 envelope unflavored gelatin
½ cup **ARROW® Coffee Flavored Brandy**
1 egg
¼ cup sugar
⅛ teaspoon salt
1 cup (6 ounces) semi-sweet chocolate morsels
1 cup heavy cream

In small saucepan, heat milk and gelatin to boiling point, stirring to dissolve gelatin. Pour into blender with remaining ingredients except cream. Process until smooth. Add cream. Process at low speed until well blended. Pour into a 1½ quart mold. Chill until firm.
Serves 8

Roquefort Puff Pastry

Thaw 2 packages (12 shells) frozen puff pastry shells. Separate each shell into 2 layers. Mash 8 oz. **ROQUEFORT Cheese** until creamy. Spread 1 tablespoon of the cheese evenly on 12 of the bottom rounds. Cover cheese with top rounds. Place on an ungreased cookie sheet. Bake in a preheated hot oven (400°F.) for 30 to 35 minutes. Serve hot.
Makes 12 servings

Favorite recipe from the **Roquefort Association, Inc.**

Ricotta Filled Puffs

½ cup shortening
⅛ teaspoon salt
1 cup sifted all-purpose flour
3 eggs
1 cup boiling water
Filling:
1 container (15 oz.) **MIGLIORE® Ricotta**
¼ cup confectioners sugar
1 teaspoon vanilla
¼ teaspoon lemon rind

Preheat oven to 450°. Add shortening and salt to 1 cup boiling water; stir over medium heat until mixture boils. Lower heat, add flour all at once and stir vigorously until mixture leaves sides of pan. Remove from heat and add 1 egg at a time, beating thoroughly after each addition. Shape on ungreased cookie sheet, using 1 teaspoon to 1 tablespoon paste per puff (depending on size desired). A pastry bag may be used. Bake 20 minutes, reduce oven temperature to 350° and bake about 20 minutes longer. Remove from oven and place on rack to cool.

Combine ricotta, confectioners sugar, vanilla and lemon rind. Blend well. Cut tops from puffs, fill with ricotta mixture, replace tops and sprinkle with confectioners sugar.

Chiquita® Frozen Yogurt Banana Dessert

⅔ cup sugar
½ cup orange juice
4 large ripe **CHIQUITA® Bananas**
2 teaspoons lemon juice
1 cup plain yogurt
2 egg whites

1. Combine sugar and orange juice in saucepan. Heat and stir until sugar is dissolved. Set aside to cool.
2. Slice bananas into blender container, add lemon juice. Whirl until bananas are pulp. Add yogurt blending well. With motor running, add orange juice mixture.
3. Pour into 9″ × 9″ flat pan and place in freezer for about two hours or until mixture is frozen to a slush.
4. Break up frozen mixture and put in mixer bowl. Beat until smooth adding egg whites one at a time. Continue beating until light and fluffy.
5. Return to pan and freeze until firm; about 1 hour.
Yield: 9-12 servings

KNOX®
Peach Melba Cake

1 envelope **KNOX® Unflavored Gelatine**
2 tablespoons sugar
1 cup boiling water
1 package (10 oz.) frozen raspberries, slightly thawed
1 can (16 oz.) sliced peaches, drained and chopped (reserve syrup)
1 container (4½ oz.) frozen whipped topping, thawed
8 or 9-inch angel food cake, cut into 1-inch cubes (about 2 qts.)

In large bowl, mix unflavored gelatine with sugar; add boiling water and stir until gelatine is completely dissolved. Stir in raspberries until melted and reserved syrup. Chill, stirring occasionally, until mixture is consistency of unbeaten egg whites. Fold in peaches, whipped topping and cake. Turn into 9-inch spring-form pan or 8-cup mold or bowl and chill until set.
Makes 8 to 10 servings

Banana Marshmallow Treats

16 graham cracker squares
¼ cup creamy peanut butter
1 small banana, peeled, sliced thin
8 **FIRESIDE Regular Marshmallows**

Arrange 8 graham cracker squares on cookie sheet; spread each with 1½ teaspoons peanut butter. Overlap 3 banana slices on top of peanut butter; put marshmallow in center. Broil 4-inches from heat, until marshmallows are lightly browned. Top with remaining crackers, pressing gently until marshmallow spreads.   *8 treats*

Chocolate-Caramel Apples

> 5 medium apples
> 5 wooden sticks or skewers
> 4 boxes (1.61 ounces each) **MILK DUDS®**
> 1 tablespoon milk
> 2 teaspoons butter
> ¾ teaspoon vanilla
> ¾ cup finely chopped walnuts

Wash and dry apples; remove stems. Insert stick into stem end of each apple; set aside. In saucepan, heat **MILK DUDS®**, milk, butter and vanilla over low heat, stirring constantly, until candy has melted and mixture is smooth. Remove from heat. Dip apples into candy mixture, one at a time, turning to coat evenly. Allow excess candy mixture to drip back into pan. Roll coated apples in nuts. Transfer to buttered cookie sheet. Let stand until firm.
5 apples

Ice Cream Desserts

EAGLE®BRAND

Easy Homemade Chocolate Ice Cream

> 1 (14-ounce) can **EAGLE® Brand Sweetened Condensed Milk** (not evaporated milk)
> ⅔ cup chocolate flavored syrup
> 2 cups (1 pint) whipping cream, whipped

In large bowl, stir together sweetened condensed milk and syrup. Fold in whipped cream. Pour into aluminum foil-lined 9 × 5-inch loaf pan; cover. Freeze 6 hours or until firm. Scoop ice cream from pan or remove from pan, peel off foil and slice. Return leftovers to freezer.   *Makes about 1½ quarts*

VARIATIONS:

COCONUT ALMOND

Omit chocolate syrup. In large bowl, combine sweetened condensed milk, 2 tablespoons water, 2 egg yolks and 4 teaspoons vanilla extract. Fold in whipped cream with ½ cup toasted flaked coconut and ½ cup toasted slivered almonds.

COFFEE

Omit chocolate syrup. In large bowl, combine sweetened condensed milk, 1 tablespoon instant coffee dissolved in 2 tablespoons water, 2 beaten egg yolks and 4 teaspoons vanilla extract. Fold in whipped cream.   *(Continued)*

FRENCH VANILLA

Omit chocolate syrup. In large bowl, combine sweetened condensed milk, 2 tablespoons water, 2 beaten egg yolks and 4 teaspoons vanilla extract. Fold in whipped cream.

LEMON

Omit chocolate syrup. In large bowl, combine sweetened condensed milk, 2 tablespoons **REALEMON® Reconstituted Lemon Juice**, 1 tablespoon grated lemon rind and few drops yellow food coloring. Fold in whipped cream.

MINT CHOCOLATE CHIP

Omit chocolate syrup. In large bowl, combine sweetened condensed milk, 2 teaspoons peppermint extract, 3 to 4 drops green food coloring and 2 tablespoons water. Fold in whipped cream and ½ cup small dark chocolate-flavored baking chips.

MOCHA

Dissolve 1 tablespoon instant coffee in 1 teaspoon hot water; combine with sweetened condensed milk and chocolate syrup. Fold in whipped cream.

RASPBERRY

Omit chocolate syrup. Thaw 1 (10-ounce) package frozen raspberries in syrup. With blender, blend until smooth. In large bowl, combine raspberries and sweetened condensed milk. Fold in whipped cream.

STRAWBERRY

Omit chocolate syrup. Thaw 1 (10-ounce) package frozen strawberries in syrup. With blender, blend strawberries until smooth. In large bowl, combine strawberries and sweetened condensed milk. Fold in whipped cream.

PEANUT BUTTER

Omit chocolate syrup. In large bowl, combine sweetened condensed milk, 2 tablespoons water, 2 beaten egg yolks and ½ cup peanut butter. Fold in whipped cream.

PEPPERMINT CANDY

Omit chocolate syrup. In large bowl, combine 2 beaten egg yolks, 2 tablespoons water, sweetened condensed milk and 4 teaspoons vanilla extract. Fold in whipped cream and ¼ cup crushed hard peppermint candy.

PEACH

Omit chocolate syrup. Drain 1 (16-ounce) can peaches. With blender, blend until smooth. In large bowl, combine peaches, sweetened condensed milk, 3 beaten egg yolks and ½ teaspoon almond extract. Fold in whipped cream.

BUTTER PECAN

Omit chocolate syrup. In small saucepan, melt 2 tablespoons butter; stir in ¼ cup chopped pecans. In large bowl, combine sweetened condensed milk, 2 beaten egg yolks, 1 teaspoon maple flavoring and buttered pecans. Fold in whipped cream.

Sealtest®

Heavenly Hash Pie

1½ cups finely crushed gingersnaps
¼ cup sugar
¼ cup butter or margarine, melted
½ of ½ gallon SEALTEST® Heavenly Hash Ice Cream, softened
Whipped cream (optional)

Measure crumbs into medium-sized mixing bowl. Toss with sugar and melted butter until well mixed. With back of spoon, press mixture to bottom and sides of 8 inch pie plate, leaving small rim. Place in moderate oven (375°) for 8 minutes. Remove to wire rack to cool completely. Spread softened Heavenly Hash ice cream evenly into prepared crust. Freeze until firm. At serving time, garnish with whipped cream if desired.

Makes 4 to 6 servings

Bits 'O Brickle® Ice Cream Pie & Sauce

Pie:
Prepared 9″ graham cracker pie shell
½ gal. vanilla ice cream, softened to spoon easily but not melted
One-half 7.8 oz. bag HEATH® BITS 'O BRICKLE®

Spoon half of softened ice cream into prepared pie shell. Sprinkle ½ bag HEATH® BITS 'O BRICKLE® on top. Heap with remaining ice cream. Freeze.

Sauce:
1½ cups sugar
1 cup evaporated milk
Remaining ½ bag HEATH® BITS 'O BRICKLE®
¼ cup butter or margarine
¼ cup light corn syrup
Dash salt

Combine sugar, milk, butter or margarine, syrup and salt. Bring to boil over low heat; boil 1 min. Remove from heat and stir in remaining HEATH® BITS 'O BRICKLE®. Cool, stirring occasionally. Chill. *To Serve:* Stir sauce well, then spoon over individual pie wedges. Remaining sauce may be refrigerated in a tightly covered container for use as a topping. *Serves eight*

Strawberry Wine Pie

Heat 1 cup ALMADÉN Mountain Nectar Vin Rosé to boiling; pour over 1 package (3 oz.) strawberry-flavored gelatin in a large bowl, stirring to dissolve. Add 1 pint softened vanilla ice cream, stirring until ice cream melts and mixture begins to set. Fold in 1 basket strawberries, rinsed and cut in halves. Spread in a cooled baked 9-inch Graham Cracker Crust* Chill until firm. Garnish with whipped cream and whole berries. *Makes 8 servings*

*Graham Cracker Crust

Mix 1 cup graham cracker crumbs, ¼ cup ground almonds, 3 tablespoons sugar and ¼ cup melted butter or margarine. Press crumb mixture evenly and firmly into a 9-inch pie pan. Bake in 400° oven for 6 to 8 minutes until browned.

Libby's Libby's Libby's

Ice Cream Pumpkin Pies

2 pints vanilla ice cream, softened
2 nine-inch packaged graham cracker crumb crusts
1 can (16 oz.) LIBBY'S® Solid Pack Pumpkin
1½ cups sugar
1 teaspoon ground cinnamon
½ teaspoon ground ginger
¼ teaspoon ground cloves
½ teaspoon salt
1 teaspoon vanilla
2 cups whipping cream
Glazed Almonds*

Spread one pint ice cream in the bottom of each crumb crust; place in freezer while making filling. In a large bowl, combine pumpkin, sugar, spices, salt and vanilla; mix well. Beat 1 cup of the cream until stiff; fold into pumpkin mixture until no streaks of white remain. Top each pie with half of the pumpkin mixture. Freeze until solid, at least 4 hours. Wrap well with foil for longer storage. To serve, remove from freezer 20 minutes before cutting. To garnish: whip ½ cup cream for each pie; spoon in a ring on pie; sprinkle with Glazed Almonds. *Yields 2 nine-inch pies*

*Glazed Almonds

In a small heavy skillet, combine 1 cup slivered blanched almonds and ¼ cup sugar. Place over medium heat, stirring constantly and rapidly to prevent burning as sugar begins to melt and turn color. When almonds are caramel color, remove from heat; spread on greased baking sheet. Break apart when cool.

Black Forest Ice Cream Cake

1 quart FRIENDLY® Golden Vanilla or Burgundy Cherry Ice Cream, softened
1¾ cups unsifted all-purpose flour
2 cups sugar
¾ cup HERSHEY'S® Cocoa
2 teaspoons baking soda
1 teaspoon baking powder
1 teaspoon salt
2 eggs
1 cup strong black coffee
1 cup buttermilk or sour milk*
½ cup vegetable oil
1 teaspoon vanilla
3 cups whipped cream
1 cup cherry pie filling

Firmly pack FRIENDLY® Ice Cream into a foil-lined 9-inch round cake pan. Cover; freeze about 2 hours. Combine flour, sugar, cocoa, baking soda, baking powder and salt in large mixer bowl. Add eggs, coffee, buttermilk, oil and vanilla. Beat on medium speed 2 minutes (batter will be thin). Pour batter into greased and floured 9-inch round cake pans. Bake at 350° for 30 to

12

35 minutes or until cake tester comes out clean. Cool 10 minutes; remove from pans and cool completely. Place 1 cake layer upside down on serving plate; top with **FRIENDLY® Ice Cream** unmolded from cake pan. Place second cake layer, top side up, over **FRIENDLY® Ice Cream** layer. Gently spread whipped cream on top and sides of cake. With decorator's tube or spoon, make border of whipped cream around edge of top layer of cake. Fill center with cherry pie filling. Cover and freeze at least 1 hour before serving.

*To sour milk: Use 1 tablespoon vinegar plus milk to equal 1 cup.

Seven-Layer Ice Cream Cake

Using a packaged cake mix, bake a 9-inch square white cake. When cold, cut cake in half, making 2 rectangles; split each into two layers. Spread one layer with **BREYERS® Chocolate Ice Cream**; one with **BREYERS® Butter Almond Ice Cream**; one with **BREYERS® Natural Strawberry Ice Cream**. Put one layer on top of the other, with a cake layer on top; pressing into shape. Wrap and freeze. Before serving, let thaw in refrigerator for about 1 hour. Slice and serve with chocolate sauce or thawed frozen strawberries.

Pie Crust

Ice Cream Sundae Pie

1 **KEEBLER® READY-CRUST® Chocolate-Flavored Pie Crust**
2 pints ice cream*
1 cup hot fudge sauce, heated
¼ cup chopped nuts
Whipped cream or topping
Maraschino cherries

Allow ice cream to soften or stir with a spoon until pliable. Spoon into crust. Cover and freeze until firm, about 3 hours. Serve pie wedges with hot fudge sauce, nuts, whipped cream or topping and cherries.

*ICE CREAM VARIATIONS:

2 pints of the same flavor such as peppermint, pistachio nut, fruit flavors, or chocolate. Or use two flavors such as chocolate and peppermint, mint-chocolate chip, fruit or nut ice creams.

Sealtest®

Blueberry Peach Charlotte

17-18 slices firm white bread
1½ quarts **SEALTEST® Peach Ice Cream**
4 cups blueberries
1 cup sugar
2 tablespoons cornstarch
½ cup water
1 teaspoon cinnamon

To make sauce, combine cornstarch, sugar and water in saucepan. Cook over medium heat until thickened. Stir in blueberries and cinnamon. Cook until blueberries are soft and sauce is thick. Cool.
Cut crusts off bread and cut slices into three pieces. Line bottom

and sides of a 2-quart soufflé dish with bread slices, fitting together so there are no empty spaces. Spoon in ⅓ of blueberry sauce and cover with half of the softened ice cream, about 3 cups. Add another layer of bread slices and another ⅓ sauce. Cover with remaining 3 cups of ice cream, and another layer of bread. Finish with remaining sauce. Freeze for 24 hours. Before serving, remove from freezer and let stand at room temperature. Run knife around outer edge of dish and turn upside down on serving platter. If desired, garnish with whipped cream and sprinkle with fresh blueberries.
12 servings

Strawberry Ice Cream Fruit Bowl

1 angel food cake
1 quart **BREYERS® Strawberry Ice Cream**
2 1-lb. cans fruit cocktail
Whipped cream (optional)

Tear half of the cake into 2-inch pieces with fingers or forks. Save remaining half for future use. Drain fruit cocktail and fold into softened ice cream. Mix in angel food cake pieces. Turn mixture into a 6-cup bowl that has been rinsed in cold water. Freeze for 5-6 hours or overnight. To serve, dip bowl in hot water for the count of 8; turn out onto a serving platter. If desired, garnish with piped whipped cream and fresh fruit.
Makes 10 servings

Note: diced fresh fruit or frozen mixed fruit (thawed and drained) may be used instead of canned.

Amaretto di Galliano

Amaretto Delight

6 to 8 large scoops of ice cream in assorted flavors
2 cups fresh fruit in season
AMARETTO di GALLIANO™
Strawberries
Whipped Cream

Heap ice cream in stemmed serving dish. Spoon fruit around scoops of ice cream. Pour about 1 ounce **AMARETTO di GALLIANO™** over each scoop of ice cream. Garnish with strawberries and whipped cream.
Serves 6 to 8

KITCHENS OF _Sara Lee_

Apple Danish a la Mode

6 frozen **SARA LEE Individual Apple Danish**
½ cup caramel topping
1 tablespoon rum
1 pint vanilla ice cream

Warm Danish according to package directions. While Danish are warming, stir together caramel topping and rum. Place Danish on plates; top each with scoop of ice cream. Pour about 1 tablespoon rum sauce over each serving.
Makes 6 servings

Praline®
Cherry Crunch

Crumble 1 pecan shortbread cookie and line bottom of demi-snifter. Add 2 to 3 tablespoons canned cherry pie filling. Top with 3 to 4 vanilla ice cream balls. Drizzle with **PRALINE® Liqueur**. Garnish with cookie crumbs and whole cherry.

Spicy Applesauce
Ice Cream Roll

3 eggs
1 cup sugar
1 can (16½ ounces) **STOKELY'S FINEST®**
  Applesauce, divided
1 cup all-purpose flour
1 teaspoon baking powder
1 teaspoon cinnamon, divided
¼ teaspoon nutmeg
¼ teaspoon salt
Confectioners sugar
1 quart vanilla ice cream, slightly softened

Preheat oven to 375°F. Line greased 15 × 10 × 1-inch jelly-roll pan with waxed paper; grease paper. In small mixing bowl, beat eggs at high speed with electric mixer 5 minutes. Gradually beat in sugar and ½ cup applesauce (reserving remaining applesauce for topping). Sift together flour, baking powder, ¾ teaspoon cinnamon, nutmeg, and salt; blend into egg mixture using low speed of mixer. Spread batter in prepared pan and bake 15 minutes, or until cake is lightly browned and springs back when pressed with fingers. Sprinkle clean dish towel with confectioners sugar. Immediately invert cake onto prepared towel. Remove waxed paper; roll cake and towel from narrow end; cool completely. Unroll cake, trim edges if desired, remove from towel, spread with softened ice cream, and reroll. Wrap tightly in foil or plastic film and freeze. Blend reserved applesauce with remaining ¼ teaspoon cinnamon; chill. When ready to serve, cut roll into 8 or 10 slices. Top each slice with applesauce mixture. *8 to 10 servings*

Tortoni
Frangelico®

1 quart pistachio ice cream, slightly softened
½ cup heavy cream, whipped
⅓ cup **FRANGELICO® Liqueur**
⅓ cup macaroon crumbs

Turn ice cream into large chilled bowl; fold in whipped cream, **FRANGELICO®**, macaroon crumbs. Spoon into chilled dessert dishes. Freeze until firm. (Garnish with macaroon crumbs if desired.) *6 to 8 servings*

Domino®
Crispy
Chocolate Ring

¼ cup butter or margarine
½ cup **DOMINO® Golden Light Brown Sugar**, firmly packed
⅓ cup peanut butter
1 envelope (1 ounce) pre-melted unsweetened chocolate flavor
3 cups crisp rice cereal or cornflakes

Melt butter in medium saucepan. Add sugar, stirring well. Add peanut butter and chocolate flavor; stir until well blended. Stir in cereal; mix until cereal is well coated. Pack mixture into well buttered 8-inch ring mold or individual ring molds. Chill until firm. Unmold by running spatula around inside of mold. Serve with ice cream balls if desired. *Makes 6 to 8 servings*

Droste® Chocolate Custard
Sauce

⅓ cup sugar
2 tablespoons unsifted flour
1 cup milk
2 egg yolks
1½ teaspoons butter
¼ cup **DROSTE® Bittersweet Chocolate Liqueur**
¼ cup heavy cream, whipped
Assorted fresh fruit

Combine sugar and flour in a medium saucepan. Gradually beat in milk. Cook over medium high heat, stirring constantly, until mixture comes to a full boil. Reduce heat to low and cook 1 minute. Stir a small amount of hot milk mixture into egg yolks, then stir yolks into milk mixture in saucepan. Cook 1 minute more, stirring constantly. Remove from heat; stir in butter. Cool mixture thoroughly. Just before serving stir in **DROSTE® Bittersweet Chocolate Liqueur**; fold in whipped cream. Serve over assorted fresh fruit. *Makes 1½ cups*

Hot Fudge Sauce

1 pkg. (10 oz.) **GHIRARDELLI® Milk Chocolate Blocks**
⅓ to ½ cup milk
1 teaspoon vanilla

In heavy saucepan, break chocolate into hot milk. Stir constantly until sauce is smooth; add vanilla. Serve warm over ice cream. *Makes 1¼ cups sauce*

MICROWAVE METHOD:
Melt chocolate with milk in measuring cup for 3-4 minutes, stirring twice; add vanilla.

Peanut Butter-Ice Cream Tarts

½ cup whipping cream
1 quart vanilla ice cream
½ cup JIF® Crunchy Peanut Butter
8 baked tart shells

Whip cream till soft peaks form. Stir ice cream to soften. Quickly fold JIF® and whipped cream into softened ice cream. Spoon into tart shells. Freeze about 5 hours or till firm. Remove from freezer 10 minutes before serving. If desired, sprinkle with chopped peanuts.

Makes 8 servings

Banana Flambé

SWIFT'S® Vanilla Ice Cream
3 tablespoons SWIFT'S BROOKFIELD® Butter
½ cup brown sugar
2 bananas
⅛ teaspoon cinnamon
3 drops brandy or rum flavoring
Sugar cubes
Lemon extract

Melt butter and brown sugar in a chafing dish. Cut each banana lengthwise and then crosswise into 4 pieces. Sauté until tender. Add cinnamon and flavoring; stir. Dip sugar cubes into lemon extract, place on top of sauce, and touch with a lighted match. (The cubes will flame for 1 to 2 minutes.) Spoon hot sauce over vanilla ice cream. Top with salted nuts, if desired.

Yield: 4 servings

Virginia Dare's Creme De Menthe Parfaits

Scoop vanilla ice cream into parfait glass. Add VIRGINIA DARE Creme De Menthe Syrup. Top with whipped cream and a maraschino cherry. Other delicious and colorful varieties: Use VIRGINIA DARE Creme De Maraschino, Claret, Chocolate Mint, Strawberry-Raspberry or Melba. For a formal dinner, use Rum, Brandy or Sherry Sauces.

Miniature Baked Alaskas

2 RAFFETTO® Grand Marnier Brandied Peaches
4 3-inch baked tart shells
2 egg whites
¼ cup sugar
½ pint vanilla ice cream

Carefully cut each peach in half and place one half in the bottom of each baked tart shell. Beat egg whites until stiff. Gradually beat in sugar, 1 tablespoonful at a time until meringue is stiff and shiny. Divide ice cream between peach halves. Cover ice cream and peaches with a layer of meringue, being careful to cover ice cream completely. Place on a baking sheet and bake in very hot preheated 450° oven 3 to 4 minutes or just until meringue is lightly browned. Remove from oven and serve immediately. *4 servings*

Note: These can be prepared and held in the freezer, then baked at the last minute just before serving. Or they can be lightly browned, then frozen and served frozen.

Baked Alaska in Patty Shells

Vanilla ice cream
1 package (10 oz.) frozen PEPPERIDGE FARM® Patty Shells, baked
Meringue*

Preheat oven to 450°. Bake Patty Shells according to package directions. Place baked Patty Shells on bread board or cookie sheet. Fill each Patty Shell with ice cream. Cover the ice cream and Patty Shell completely with meringue. Bake in 450° oven for five minutes or until delicately browned. Serve immediately.

*Meringue

Beat the whites of two eggs until frothy. Gradually beat in four tablespoons granulated sugar. Continue beating until stiff. Flavor with ¼ teaspoon vanilla.

Baked Alaska

Sponge angel food or pound loaf cake
1 quart LOUIS SHERRY® Ice Cream (your favorite flavor)
4 egg whites
⅛ teaspoon cream of tartar
⅛ teaspoon salt
½ cup sugar
½ teaspoon vanilla

Cover two thicknesses of corrugated cardboard, 8 × 6 inches, with aluminum foil. Cut enough ½″ thick slices of cake to construct a rectangle 7 × 5 inches. Place cake on foil and freeze.

Let egg whites stand at room temperature for 1 hour. Beat egg whites until frothy. Add cream of tartar and salt; continue beating until soft peaks form when beater is slowly raised. Gradually beat in sugar, 2 tablespoons at a time, beating well after each addition. Add vanilla and continue beating for about 3 minutes.

Place ice cream on cake base. Quickly spread ice cream and cake with meringue, spreading down onto foil all around to seal completely. Make swirls on top and sides. Place the Alaska on a cookie sheet and bake at 500° for about 3 minutes or until meringue is light brown. Remove to chilled platter. Serve at once.

Serves 12 to 16

THE CHRISTIAN BROTHERS®
Napa Sherbet

1 envelope plain gelatine
½ cup cold water
2 cups **THE CHRISTIAN BROTHERS® Napa Rosé**
¾ cup sugar
¼ cup lime juice, freshly squeezed
1 package (10 oz.) frozen raspberries

Mix gelatine and water; let stand to soften gelatine. Meanwhile, heat wine until piping hot but not boiling. Stir in sugar to dissolve. Stir in gelatine mixture until dissolved. Mix in lime juice and raspberries. Place in freezer until softly frozen. Turn into mixer bowl. Beat vigorously just until frothy and berries are evenly blended. Freeze solid. *Makes 1 quart*

Karo®
Cantaloupe Sherbet

1 envelope unflavored gelatin
½ cup milk
3 cups cubed cantaloupe
1 cup **KARO® Light Corn Syrup**

In small saucepan sprinkle gelatin over milk. Stir over low heat until dissolved. Place in blender container with cantaloupe and corn syrup; cover. Blend on high speed 30 seconds. Pour into 9 × 9 × 2-inch pan. Cover; freeze overnight. Soften slightly at room temperature, about 15 mintues. Spoon into large bowl. With mixer at low speed, beat until smooth, but not melted. Pour into 4-cup mold or freezer container. Cover; freeze about 4 hours or until firm. Unmold or soften at room temperature for easier scooping. *Makes about 4 cups*

VARIATIONS:

Blueberry Sherbet

Follow recipe for Cantaloupe Sherbet. Omit cantaloupe. Use 3 cups whole blueberries. *Makes about 3½ cups*

Honeydew Sherbet

Follow recipe for Cantaloupe Sherbet. Omit cantaloupe. Use 3 cups cubed honeydew melon. *Makes about 4 cups*

Nectarine Sherbet

Follow recipe for Cantaloupe Sherbet. Omit cantaloupe. Use 3 cups cubed nectarines and 1 tablespoon lemon juice. *Makes about 4 cups*

Papaya Sherbet

Follow recipe for Cantaloupe Sherbet. Omit cantaloupe. Use 3 cups cubed papaya and 1 tablespoon lemon juice. *Makes about 4 cups*

Peach Sherbet

Follow recipe for Cantaloupe Sherbet. Omit cantaloupe. Use 3 cups cubed peaches and 1 tablespoon lemon juice. *Makes about 4 cups*

Pineapple Sherbet

Follow recipe for Cantaloupe Sherbet. Omit cantaloupe. Use 3 cups cubed pineapple. *Makes about 4 cups*

Strawberry Sherbet

Follow recipe for Cantaloupe Sherbet. Omit cantaloupe. Use 3 cups whole strawberries. *Makes about 3½ cups*

Watermelon Sherbet

Follow recipe for Cantaloupe Sherbet. Omit cantaloupe. Use 3 cups cubed watermelon. *Makes about 4 cups*

Ginger Ale Sherbet

Follow recipe for Cantaloupe Sherbet. Omit cantaloupe. Use 1 can (16 oz) sliced peaches, drained, 2 cups ginger ale, and 1 tablespoon chopped crystallized ginger. *Makes about 4 cups*

Raspberry-Peach Sherbet

Follow recipe for Cantaloupe Sherbet. Omit cantaloupe. Use 2 cups sliced peaches and 1 cup raspberries.

REALEMON®
Creamy Lemon Sherbet

1 cup sugar
2 cups (1 pint) **BORDEN® Whipping Cream** whipped
½ cup **REALEMON® Lemon Juice From Concentrate**
Few drops yellow food coloring

In medium bowl, combine sugar and cream, stirring until dissolved. Stir in **REALEMON®** and fool coloring. Pour into 8-inch square pan or directly into sherbert dishes. Freeze 3 hours or until firm. Remove from freezer 5 minutes before serving. Return leftovers to freezer. *Makes about 3 cups*

VARIATION:

Lime Sherbet

Substitute **REALIME® Lime Juice From Concentrate** for **REALEMON®** and green food coloring for yellow.

METAXA®
The spirit that is Greece
Manto Melon Freeze

4 cups 1-inch cubes ripe cantaloupe
1 envelope unflavored gelatin
⅓ cup **METAXA® Manto Liqueur**
2 tablespoons lemon juice
¼ boiling water
1 cup heavy cream
¼ cup sugar

Puree cantaloupe in food processor or blender. Soften gelatin in **METAXA® Manto Liqueur** and lemon juice. Stir in boiling water. Stir gelatin mixture into pureed cantaloupe.

Beat heavy cream with sugar until stiff peaks form. Fold into cantaloupe mixture. Place in freezer, stirring occasionally as mixture begins to freeze. Freeze 3 to 4 hours until very firm. Allow mixture to stand at room temperature about 5 minutes before serving. Scoop into individual dessert dishes; garnish as desired.

Makes 8 servings

Kiwi Emerald Ice

1 pound **New Zealand Kiwifruit** (about 5 to 6 medium)
1 cup sugar
1 cup water
¼ cup lemon juice

Peel and quarter kiwifruit. Beat with electric mixer until coarsely mashed. Measure 1½ cups mashed fruit; stir in sugar and let stand 10 to 15 minutes to dissolve sugar. Stir in water and lemon juice. Pour mixture into 8-inch cake pan; freeze until mixture is just firm but not hard. Turn into mixing bowl; beat at high speed until smooth. Return to freezer; freeze firm. To serve: remove from freezer and let stand 10 to 15 minutes to soften slightly. Scoop or spoon into individual serving dishes.   *Makes about 3½ cups*

Favorite recipe from the **New Zealand Kiwifruit Authority**

Coupes Napoléon

2 seedless oranges
3 tablespoons **MANDARINE NAPOLÉON**
1 pint lemon sherbet, slightly softened

Halve oranges and lift out segments, using the tip of a grapefruit spoon. Clean out inside of shells and refrigerate. Marinate orange segments in **MANDARINE NAPOLÉON**. Stir 3 tablespoons of marinade into softened sherbet, then pile into reserved orange shells. Freeze until firm. Garnish with orange segments.

4 servings

Lemon Ice

1½ cups water
1 cup sugar
½ cup **BERTOLLI® Soave Classico Wine**
Grated rind of 4 lemons
¾ to 1 cup lemon juice

Heat water and sugar to boiling in saucepan; boil 3 minutes. Cool. Mix all ingredients. Freeze in 9-inch pan until firm, about 3 hours.

Dry Sack® Citrus Italian Ice

1 cup water
¼ cup sugar
2 cups orange juice
¾ cup lemon juice
½ cup lime juice
3 tablespoons **DRY SACK® Sherry**

Combine water and sugar in a saucepan; heat over low heat until sugar dissolves. Combine orange, lemon and lime juices, **DRY SACK® Sherry** and prepared sugar-water mixture in a large metal bowl. Freeze until crystals form around edges and over top of mixture, about 1½ hours. Beat well with a spoon or hand beater. Continue freezing and beating until mixture is icy and mounding. Serve in chilled dessert glasses and garnished with fresh fruit or mint leaves if desired.   *Makes 6 cups*

Puddings

ARGO®/KINGSFORD'S® Chocolate Pudding Mix

4 cups nonfat dry milk powder
2⅔ cups sugar
1⅓ cups **ARGO®/KINGSFORD'S® Corn Starch**
1 cup unsweetened cocoa
½ teaspoon salt

In large bowl stir together dry milk, sugar, corn starch, cocoa and salt until well mixed. Store in tightly covered container at room temperature.   *Makes about 7 cups*

Note: Stir pudding mix before each use.

Chocolate Pudding

1 cup Chocolate Pudding Mix
2 cups water
1 tablespoon **MAZOLA®/NUCOA® Margarine**
½ teaspoon vanilla

In medium saucepan stir together pudding mix and water until well mixed. Stirring constantly, bring to boil over medium heat and boil 1 minute. Stir in margarine and vanilla. Pour into individual serving dishes. Cover; refrigerate.

Makes 4 (½ cup) servings

VARIATIONS:

Mocha Pudding

Follow recipe for Chocolate Pudding. Substitute 1 cup strong black coffee for 1 cup of the water.

Choco-Peppermint Pudding

Follow recipe for Chocolate Pudding. Add ¼ teaspoon peppermint extract with margarine and vanilla. Top chilled pudding with ¼ cup crushed peppermint candy.

Nutty Chocolate Pudding

Follow recipe for Chocolate Pudding. Mix ¼ cup **SKIPPY® Creamy** or **Super Chunk Peanut Butter** with the water until smooth. Top chilled pudding with ¼ cup chopped peanuts.

Lemon Pudding With a Twist

2 envelopes unflavored gelatin
⅓ cup fresh lemon juice
1 (12 oz.) can **DIET SHASTA® Creme Soda**
1½ teaspoons grated lemon peel
2 cups buttermilk
1½ teaspoons artificial sweetener
4 or 5 drops yellow food coloring
Fresh strawberries for decoration

Combine gelatin and lemon juice in blender top. Heat **DIET SHASTA® Creme Soda** to boiling. Pour over gelatin and whirl until dissolved. Blend in remaining ingredients. Pour into serving dishes. Chill until set. Garnish each serving with a fresh berry.

Makes about 1 quart

Rich Chocolate Pudding

2¾ cups milk
¼ cup MALT-O-MEAL®
2 squares unsweetened chocolate
2 egg yolks
½ cup sugar
¼ tsp. salt
¼ tsp. cinnamon
½ cup chopped nuts
¾ tsp. vanilla

In medium saucepan, heat milk. Add MALT-O-MEAL® gradually. Cook until thickened. Add chocolate; stir until melted and blended. Cook at low heat for 10 minutes, stirring occasionally. Combine remaining ingredients in a small bowl. Add slowly to cooked mixture and continue cooking for 2 minutes. Pour into greased 1 quart casserole and bake at 350° for 15 minutes. Serve warm.   *4 to 6 servings*

Mueller's.

Upside Down Noodle Kugel
(Pudding)

¼ cup parve margarine, softened
½ cup light brown sugar
8 slices canned pineapple, well drained
2 eggs
¼ cup cooking oil or melted parve margarine
¼ cup sugar
½ teaspoon salt
½ teaspoon cinnamon
1 tablespoon lemon juice
½ teaspoon grated lemon rind
8 ounces (5½ to 6 cups) MUELLER'S® Fine Egg Noodles
½ cup finely cut dried fruits (apricots, prunes, dates, etc.)
½ cup raisins
½ cup chopped nuts

Prepare a 9-inch ring mold or 9-inch square pan by spreading with margarine to coat thoroughly; sprinkle with brown sugar. Cut pineapple slices in half; arrange in a design on sugar mixture. In large bowl, beat eggs and oil with sugar, salt, cinnamon, lemon juice and rind. Meanwhile, cook noodles 5 to 6 minutes; drain and stir into egg mixture. Add dried fruits, raisins and nuts; toss to distribute throughout. Carefully spoon into prepared pan so as not to dislodge pineapple slices. Bake at 350°F. for 40 to 50 minutes or until set and golden brown. Let stand 5 minutes; loosen with spatula and invert over warm serving dish.   *6 to 8 servings*

Note: A good side dish with chicken or beef. Or, as dessert with Pineapple* or Wine Sauce.**

*Pineapple Sauce

1 egg, separated
1 cup pineapple juice drained from canned pineapple
1 tablespoon lemon juice
1 tablespoon grated lemon rind

In top of double boiler, beat egg yolk; stir in pineapple juice, lemon juice and rind. Place over hot water; cook, stirring con-

stantly until thickened. Cool. Beat egg white until stiff but not dry; fold into sauce.   *Makes about 1½ cups sauce*

Note: For an extra treat, just before serving, fold in cut up fruits or berries (drain first if using canned).

**Wine Sauce

¼ cup sugar
2 tablespoons cornstarch
½ cup water
1 cup sweet red wine
1 teaspoon lemon juice

In small pan, combine sugar and cornstarch; stir in water to form a smooth paste. Cook over low heat, stirring constantly until thickened. Blend in wine and lemon juice. Cook 2 minutes, stirring constantly; do not boil.   *Makes about 1¼ cups sauce*

Custard Noodle Pudding

2 quarts water
2 teaspoons salt
1 tablespoon oil
3 eggs
2 cups milk
1 cup sugar
1½ teaspoons vanilla
4 cups AMERICAN BEAUTY® Fine Egg Noodles
¼ cup raisins
1 teaspoon nutmeg
Whipping cream, if desired

Heat oven to 350°F. Boil water in large deep pot with salt and oil (to prevent boiling over). Add noodles; stir to separate. Cook uncovered after water returns to a full rolling boil for 4 to 5 minutes. Stir occasionally. Drain and rinse under cold water.

Grease 13 × 9-inch pan. In large bowl, beat eggs. Add milk, sugar and vanilla. Stir in cooked noodles and raisins. Turn mixture into prepared pan. Sprinkle nutmeg over top. Cover and bake at 350°F. for 55 to 60 minutes or until knife inserted near center comes out clean. Serve with whipped cream, if desired.

8 to 10 servings

High Altitude—Above 3500 Feet: Cooking times may need to be increased slightly for noodles; no additional changes.

NUTRITION INFORMATION PER SERVING			
SERVING SIZE: ⅒ of recipe			
Calories	244	PERCENT U.S. RDA PER SERVING	
Protein	7 g	Protein	10
Carbohydrate	42 g	Vitamin A	6
Fat	6 g	Vitamin C	—
Sodium	78 mg	Thiamine	9
Potassium	149 mg	Riboflavin	11
		Niacin	5
		Calcium	8
		Iron	6

SUE BEE HONEY
Honey Custard

3 eggs
¼ teaspoon salt
¼ cup SUE BEE® Honey
2 cups milk, scalded
Nutmeg

Beat eggs slightly; add salt. Blend honey into hot milk. Stir milk mixture slowly into beaten eggs. Pour into five custard cups.

(Continued)

Sprinkle nutmeg over top. Arrange custard cups in shallow pan of hot water. Bake at 325° for about 30 minutes or until knife inserted in center of custard comes out clean. *Makes five servings*

HEARTLAND®
Baked Cereal Custard

1 tall can (1⅔ cups) PET® Evaporated Milk
1 cup water
1 cup HEARTLAND® Natural Cereal, Raisin Variety
2 eggs
¼ cup sugar
¼ teaspoon salt
¼ teaspoon nutmeg
1 teaspoon vanilla

1. Heat evaporated milk, water and cereal to boiling.
2. Beat eggs. Add sugar, salt, nutmeg and vanilla.
3. Gradually stir in hot cereal mixture.
4. Pour into 1½-quart casserole dish. Place casserole dish into a baking dish with an inch of water.
5. Bake in 325°F oven for 1 hour or until knife inserted near edge comes out clean. Serve warm with cream or ice cream.

Makes 6 servings, ½ cup each

Chocolate Custard
(Low Calorie)

2 cups reconstituted ALBA Instant Non-Fat Dry Milk
3 envelopes ALBA '66 Hot Cocoa Mix
3 eggs
½ teaspoon vanilla

In a small bowl, combine milk, ALBA '66, eggs and vanilla. Stir until ALBA is completely dissolved. Pour mixture into 5 custard cups. Set cups in a baking pan. Pour hot water into pan to a 1 inch level. Bake in oven preheated to 350°F for 30 minutes. Turn off heat. Allow custard to stand in oven 15 minutes. Remove from oven, cool to room temperature, cover with plastic wrap and chill.

Calories: Each serving contains approximately 119

Lemon Pudding*
(Low Calorie)

1 envelope unflavored gelatin
½ cup boiling water
1 tablespoon lemon juice
½ teaspoon grated lemon rind
¼ cup cold water
1 envelope Vanilla ALBA '77
6 oz. net weight of WEIGHT WATCHERS® Vanilla
 Frozen Dessert (approx. 1¼ cups)

Stir gelatin into boiling water until dissolved. Mix in lemon juice and rind; cool slightly. In mixing bowl, beat ALBA '77 with cold water until frothy. Add WEIGHT WATCHERS® Frozen Dessert and beat on high speed with electric mixer. Slowly pour in gelatin mixture while continuing to beat until mixture is fluffy. Pour into dessert glasses and serve at once.

Calories: Each serving equals about 146

*WEIGHT WATCHERS® members should omit for each serving: ½ cup skim milk, ½ serving milk substitute, 1 serving non-citrus fruit and 1 serving extras from their menu plan.

Grape-Glazed Steamed Pudding

½ cup butter or margarine
1½ cups SMUCKER'S Grape Jelly
2 large eggs
1 cup whole-wheat flour, stirred before measuring
¾ cup all-purpose flour, stirred before measuring
¼ cup wheat germ
2½ teaspoons baking powder
1 teaspoon pumpkin or apple pie spice*
½ teaspoon salt
½ cup milk
½ cup chopped walnuts
½ cup seedless raisins

Generously grease and lightly flour 1½-quart brioche pan or steamed pudding mold. In large bowl, beat butter until fluffy. Beat in 1¼ cups Grape Jelly. Add eggs and beat until well mixed. Add whole-wheat and all-purpose flours, wheat germ, baking powder, spice, salt and milk. Beat on low speed just until mixed. Beat on medium speed until fluffy. Fold in walnuts and raisins. Spoon into prepared pan. Cover tightly with greased foil.

Meanwhile, in large saucepan, place rack in about 3 inches water. Cover and bring to a boil. Place pan on rack. Add more boiling water, if necessary, to come halfway up side of pan. Cover, reduce heat and steam about 1½ hours or until skewer inserted in center comes out clean. Remove pudding from saucepan. Let pudding stand in pan on rack 5 minutes. Loosen pudding around edge of pan. Invert onto serving plate; remove pan. In small saucepan, heat remaining ¼ cup Grape Jelly until melted. Brush over pudding to glaze. Garnish top with walnut halves, if desired. *8 servings*

*Or your own blend of ground cinnamon, nutmeg, cloves and allspice.

Peach Cottage Pudding

1 can (29 oz.) sliced peaches
¼ cup chopped nuts
½ cup LOG CABIN® Syrup
2 tablespoons MINUTE® Tapioca
¼ cup butter or margarine
½ cup sugar
1 egg
1 teaspoon vanilla
½ teaspoon ginger
¼ teaspoon nutmeg
1½ cups LOG CABIN® Regular Pancake and
 Waffle Mix
½ cup milk

Drain peaches, reserving ¾ cup of the syrup. Place peaches in well-greased 9-inch square baking dish and sprinkle with nuts. Combine measured peach syrup with ½ cup syrup and the tapioca. Pour over peaches; set aside. Cream butter. Gradually beat in sugar. Add egg, vanilla and spices, beating until well blended. Add pancake mix alternately with milk, beating after each addition until smooth. Carefully spread over peach mixture. Bake at 350° for 45 to 55 minutes or until cake tester inserted into center of cake comes out clean. Serve warm with additional pancake and waffle syrup, if desired.

All-Time Favorite Puff Pudding

¼ cup butter or margarine
½ cup sugar
1 teaspoon grated lemon rind
2 egg yolks
3 tablespoons lemon juice
2 tablespoons all-purpose flour
¼ cup **POST® GRAPE-NUTS® Brand Cereal**
1 cup milk
2 egg whites, stiffly beaten

Thoroughly cream butter with sugar and lemon rind. Add egg yolks; beat until light and fluffy. Blend in lemon juice, flour, cereal and milk. (Mixture will look curdled, but this will not affect finished product.) Fold in beaten egg whites. Pour into greased 1-quart baking dish; place the dish in pan of hot water. Bake at 325° for 1 hour and 15 minutes or until top springs back when lightly touched. When done, pudding has a cakelike layer on top with custard below. Serve warm or cold with cream or prepared whipped topping, if desired.

Makes 6 servings

Extra Nice Rice Pudding

(Low Calorie/Low Cholesterol)

1 pkg. (53 grams) **ESTEE® Vanilla Pudding**
2 cups skim milk
1 cup cooked rice
¼ cup raisins (optional)
¼ tsp. cinnamon
¼ tsp. vanilla

Prepare **ESTEE® Vanilla Pudding** with skim milk as directed on package. Cool 5 minutes. Stir in rice, raisins, and vanilla. Pour into individual serving dishes. Sprinkle top of each with cinnamon. Refrigerate until served.

Makes 6 servings, ½ cup per serving

NUTRITION INFORMATION
Calories	Carbohydrates	Protein	Cholesterol	Sodium
92	20g	4g	1mg	44mg

DIABETIC EXCHANGE INFORMATION
Bread
1½

Hydrox® Butterscotch Pudding

1 package butterscotch pudding mix
18 **HYDROX® Cookies**

Prepare butterscotch pudding as package directs. Place 1 **HYDROX® Cookie** in the bottom of each of six 6-ounce custard cups. Pour enough hot pudding over the cookies to cover them. Repeat, alternating cookies and pudding until cookies and pudding are all used. Chill at least 4 hours, or overnight. Serve in custard cups topped with whipped cream, or unmold into dessert dishes and serve with light cream, maple syrup or whipped cream.

Yield: 6 servings

Pudding in a Cloud

2 cups or 1 container (4 oz.) **BIRDS EYE® COOL WHIP® Non-Dairy Whipped Topping**, thawed
1 package (4 serving size) **JELL-O® Brand Instant Pudding and Pie Filling**, any flavor
2 cups cold milk

Divide whipped topping among 6 dessert glasses, using about ⅓ cup in each. With the back of a spoon, make a depression in the center and spread topping up the sides of the glasses. Prepare pudding mix with milk as directed on package for pudding. Spoon pudding mixture into glasses. Chill. Garnish as desired.

Makes about 3½ cups or 6 servings

Bays® English Muffin Bread Pudding

4 **BAYS® English Muffins**, cubed
2 tablespoons unsalted butter
4 cups milk, scalded
4 eggs
1½ teaspoons vanilla extract
¾ cup sugar
½ cup raisins
1½ teaspoons ground cinnamon
¼ teaspoon ground clove
¼ cup sugar

Preheat oven to 350°. Place large roasting pan with ½ inch water in oven during preheating to prepare water bath for pudding. Grease a 1½ quart **Pyrex®** pan; set aside. Place cubed muffins and butter in a bowl. Pour scalded milk over and stir to combine well. Let soak for 15 minutes, stirring occasionally. In another bowl, combine eggs, vanilla extract, sugar and raisins. Beat well to mix. Add the egg mixture to the muffin and milk mixture; stir well. Pour into prepared pan. In a small bowl, combine cinnamon, cloves and sugar. Sprinkle this mixture over the pudding. Bake in water bath for 1 hour or until the pudding is puffed and an inserted knife comes out clean. Let pudding cool for another hour or until warm. Serve with whipped cream or plain cream.

(Serves 8)

Macaroon Peasant Pudding

½ cup uncooked medium **WOLFF'S® Kasha**
1 Tbsp. melted butter or margarine
2 cups milk, scalded
2 eggs, separated
¼ cup light or unsulphured molasses
2 Tbsp. sugar
½ tsp. salt
¼ tsp. ginger
¼ tsp. nutmeg
¼ tsp. cinnamon
½ cup raisins or diced mixed fruit

Mix together kasha and melted butter. Scald milk in saucepan; stir in kasha and cook over low heat for 15-20 minutes or until kasha is tender. Beat egg yolks until lemon-colored. Add small amount of hot mixture to egg yolks, then combine egg yolks with kasha. Add molasses, sugar, salt, and spices. Stir in raisins or fruit. Beat egg whites until they form soft peaks, then gently fold in. Bake pudding in well-oiled 1-quart casserole at 325°F for 35-45 minutes or until pudding is puffy and no longer runny in center. Serve warm with whipped topping, stirred custard, or "pour" cream.

Makes 6 servings

MICROWAVE METHOD:
Kasha/milk mixture may be micro-cooked on medium power for 8-9 minutes in large measuring pitcher or bowl. Pudding may be "baked" in microwave oven on medium power for 10-15 minutes or until set. Pudding may be micro-cooked in 3-4 minutes if baked in individual custard-size cups. Arrange cups in circular pattern, turning once after 1 minute. Do not oil casserole or custard cups if micro-cooking.

Fruit Desserts

LAWRY'S

Fruit Tostada With Cream Cheese

- 2 packages (8 oz. *each*) cream cheese, softened
- 2 tablespoons grated orange rind
- 2 to 3 tablespoons sugar
- 3 tablespoons orange juice
- 2 oranges, peeled and cubed
- 1 cup halved strawberries
- 1 kiwi, peeled, halved and sliced
- 1 banana, peeled and sliced*
- 1 can (20 oz.) pineapple chunks, drained
- 1 cup shredded coconut
- 1 box LAWRY'S® Tostada Shells

In medium bowl, blend together cream cheese, orange rind, sugar and orange juice; chill. Combine cut-up fruit, pineapple and coconut; chill. Heat Tostada Shells according to package directions. Spread cream cheese mixture on Tostada Shells; top with fruit. Serve immediately. *Makes 10 servings*

*To prevent banana from browning, toss lightly in pineapple juice.

 AZTECA®

Delicate Dessert Tortillas

Dry at least ½ hour in open air:

6" AZTECA® Flour Tortillas cut into quarters

Fry in hot oil until golden and crisp. Drain on paper towels.

VARIATIONS:
Sugar and Spice

Mix ¼ cup sugar and ½ tsp. cinnamon. Sprinkle on warm tortillas.

(Continued)

Honey and Spice

Drizzle honey on warm tortillas and sprinkle with cinnamon.

Brunch Style

Sprinkle warm tortillas with powdered sugar. Use to dip into melted apricot or other fruit preserves.

Dessert Fruit Taco

- 2 cups melon balls or cubes (cantaloupe, watermelon, honeydew)
- 2 cups strawberries, washed, hulled and halved
- 2 cups pineapple chunks
- 1 cup seedless green grapes, halved
- 1 orange, peeled, sectioned and sliced into ½-inch pieces
- 1 banana, peeled and sliced
- 1 kiwi, peeled and sliced
- ½ cup fresh raspberries
- 1 box (10 shells) LAWRY'S® Super Taco Shells*
- ¼ cup powdered sugar
- ¼ teaspoon cinnamon
- Shredded coconut, to garnish

Combine all fruit in large bowl; chill. Sift together powdered sugar and cinnamon. Heat Taco Shells according to package directions. Lightly sift sugar mixture over inside and outside of heated Taco Shells. Fill each shell with 1 cup mixed fruit; garnish with coconut. *Makes 10 Super Tacos*

*May use LAWRY'S® Taco Shells, regular size. Fill regular shells with ⅓ cup mixed fruit.

STOKELY VAN CAMP

Warm Fruitful Compote

- ½ cup whole cranberry sauce
- 1 can (16 ounces) STOKELY'S FINEST® Sliced Cling Peaches, drained
- 1 can (16 ounces) STOKELY'S FINEST® Sliced Bartlett Pears, drained
- 1 can (16 ounces) STOKELY'S FINEST® Apricot Halves, drained
- 2 tablespoons sugar
- ¼ teaspoon cinnamon
- ⅛ teaspoon cloves
- ⅛ teaspoon nutmeg
- Whipped cream or frozen whipped topping (optional)
- Walnut halves (optional)

In large skillet, heat cranberry sauce. Add peaches, pears, and apricots. Sprinkle with sugar, cinnamon, cloves, and nutmeg. Cover and heat 5 to 10 minutes, or until fruit is warmed through. Stir gently to blend flavors. Serve warm garnished with nuts and whipped cream or whipped topping. *6 to 8 servings*

MICROWAVE METHOD:
Microcook cranberry sauce in 1½-quart casserole for 1½ minutes, uncovered. Add peaches, pears, and apricots. Sprinkle with sugar, cinnamon, cloves, and nutmeg. Microcook 2 minutes, uncovered. Stir mixture thoroughly but gently. Cover and microcook 1 additional minute. Serve warm, garnished with nuts and whipped cream or whipped topping.

Fruit Compote
(Low Calorie)

1 (12 oz.) can **DIET SHASTA®** Citrus Mist
1 cup diced fresh pineapple
2 cups diced apple
½ cup diced pear
Dash salt
1 cinnamon stick
½ cup diced or sectioned orange

Combine **DIET SHASTA®** with pineapple, apple, pear, salt and cinnamon. Simmer 5 minutes. Remove from heat, discard cinnamon and add orange. Serve warm or cold.   *Makes 4 or 5 servings*

Calories: 132 per serving

Three-Fruit Compote

1 can (1 pound, 1 ounce size) peaches
1 can (1 pound, 1-ounce size) apricots
1 can (1 pound, 1-ounce size) Bing cherries
1 cup **GIROUX®** Grenadine
Grated rind and juice ½ lemon

Drain syrup from all three fruits. Combine fruits with all remaining ingredients in a suitable serving dish. Chill.   *Serves about 6*

Marinated Fruit Bowl

1 pint strawberries, sliced
1½ cups seedless green grapes
1 cup honeydew balls
2 kiwis, peeled and sliced
2 oranges, peeled and sliced
1 apple, cored and sliced
2 bananas, peeled and sliced
¼ cup **HIRAM WALKER Triple Sec** liqueur
2 tablespoons honey
1 tablespoon lime juice
Mint leaves

Mix all fruits, except bananas, in large bowl. Blend **HIRAM WALKER Triple Sec**, honey and lime juice; pour over fruit and toss. Refrigerate about 2 hours. Just before serving, add bananas. Mix well. Garnish with mint leaves.   *8 to 10 servings*

Note: Any combination of fresh seasonal fruits can be used. Also, equally delicious marinated with **HIRAM WALKER Amaretto**.

Minty Orange Grape Compote
(Low Calorie)

⅓ cup honey or light corn syrup
2 tablespoons fresh squeezed lemon juice
1 to 2 tablespoons chopped fresh mint
2 **SUNKIST®** oranges, peeled, sliced into cartwheels, quartered
2 cups seedless green grapes

In bowl, combine honey, lemon juice, and mint. Add orange pieces and grapes; stir well. Chill at least 2 hours, stirring occasionally. Garnish with fresh mint sprigs, if desired.
Makes 6 servings

Calories: about 115 per ½ cup serving

Poached Pears With Raspberry Sauce

2 cups **WELCH'S®** White Grape Juice
1 cup sugar
Juice of one lemon
6 firm pears
10-ounce package frozen raspberries, partially thawed

In a large saucepan, combine white grape juice, sugar and lemon juice. Bring to a boil. Peel pears leaving stems on but removing end cores. Put into boiling syrup. Cover, reduce heat and simmer until tender. Remove from syrup and chill. When ready to serve, whirl raspberries in blender. Serve on pears.

Makes 6 servings

Pears With Raspberry Sauce

1 cup fresh or frozen raspberries
5 tablespoons of **CANADA DRY®** Club Soda
1 teaspoon granulated sugar
1 17 ounce can pear halves, chilled and drained

Put raspberries, Club Soda and sugar into a blender. Cover and blend for 30-60 seconds at high speed until pureed. Serve over pear halves.   *Makes 4-6 servings*

Wisconsin Baked Apples

6 large baking apples (about 4 pounds)
½ cup **DROMEDARY** Chopped Dates
¼ cup chopped walnuts
½ teaspoon ground cinnamon
2 tablespoons butter or margarine
1 cup water
1 (4⅝-ounce) can **SNACK MATE Cheddar** or **American Pasteurized Process Cheese Spread**

1. Preheat oven to 350°F.; lightly grease 2-quart shallow baking dish. Slice ½ inch from top of each apple; core each apple to within ½ inch of bottom.
2. In medium bowl, combine **DROMEDARY Dates**, walnuts and cinnamon; spoon into apple centers. Dot top of filling with butter or margarine.
3. Place apples in baking dish; add water. Bake, uncovered, 40 to 50 minutes, basting occasionally. Apples should be tender when pierced with cake tester. Cool slightly; top with swirl of **SNACK MATE Cheese**.   *Makes 6 servings*

MICROWAVE METHOD:
1. Prepare apples as directed in Steps 1 and 2. Place in 2-quart microwave-proof shallow baking dish. *Do not* add water.

2. Microwave, uncovered, at 100% power 16 to 18 minutes, rotating a half turn every 4 minutes. Apples should be tender when pierced with cake tester. Cool and serve as in Step 3.

 Ralston Purina Company

Apple Betty

4 cups cored and thinly sliced cooking apples
1 tablespoon lemon juice
⅔ cup packed brown sugar
⅓ cup all-purpose flour
½ teaspoon cinnamon
¼ teaspoon nutmeg
1½ cups **BRAN CHEX® Cereal** crushed to ¾ cup
⅓ cup butter or margarine, melted

Preheat oven to 375°. Butter 9-inch pie plate. Place apples in pie plate. Sprinkle with lemon juice. Thoroughly combine sugar, flour, cinnamon and nutmeg. Stir in **BRAN CHEX®** crumbs. Add butter. Mix until crumbly. Stir ¾ cup **CHEX®** mixture into apples. Arrange evenly in pie plate. Sprinkle remaining mixture over apples. Bake 25-30 minutes or until apples are tender and topping is browned. Serve warm.   *Makes 6 servings*

Note: Raisins make a nice addition. Stir into apples.

 QUAKER

Individual Apple-Oat Crisp

Base:
1 cup thin apple slices
1 tablespoon firmly packed brown sugar
1 teaspoon all-purpose flour
½ teaspoon lemon juice

Topping:
⅓ cup **QUAKER® Oats** (quick or old fashioned, uncooked)
1 tablespoon firmly packed brown sugar
1 tablespoon chopped almonds
1 teaspoon all-purpose flour
¼ teaspoon cinnamon
⅛ teaspoon nutmeg
Dash of salt
2 tablespoons butter or margarine, melted

FOR BASE:
Heat oven to 375°F. Combine all ingredients, mixing well. Place in small individual baking dish.

FOR TOPPING:
Combine dry ingredients; mix well. Add butter; mix until crumbly. Sprinkle over fruit mixture. Bake about 20 minutes or until apples are tender and topping is golden brown.
Makes 1 serving

Note: Recipe may easily be doubled to make 2 servings.

MICROWAVE METHOD:
Prepare 1 serving as recipe directs. Cook at HIGH 4½ to 5½ minutes, rotating dish ¼ turn after 3 minutes of cooking.

 Estee

Oatmeal Apple Crisp
(Low Calorie/Low Sodium)

4 medium apples, pared & sliced (about 4 cups)
20 **ESTEE® Oatmeal-Raisin Cookies** (about ½ box)
¼ cup water
1 tsp. lemon juice
1 Tbsp. flour
¼ cup **ESTEE® Granulated Fructose**
1 tsp. soft tub margarine
½ tsp. cinnamon

Preheat oven to 350°F. Arrange half of the sliced apples in the bottom of an ungreased 8″ square pan. Cover with a layer of cookies. Top with remaining sliced apples. Mix water and lemon juice together and drizzle over apples. Mix flour, **ESTEE® Fructose**, margarine, and cinnamon together until crumbly. Sprinkle evenly over top layer. Bake for 45 minutes. Best when served warm.   *Makes 16 servings, 1 2″ square per serving*

NUTRITION INFORMATION
Calories	Carbohydrates	Protein	Sodium
50	9g	1g	6mg

DIABETIC EXCHANGE INFORMATION
Fruit
1½

LAIRD'S
Brandied Fruit

1 cup water
1 cup sugar
1 cup **LAIRD'S APPLEJACK**

Combine water and sugar; bring to a boil and add **LAIRD'S APPLEJACK**. Cool. Serve over any desired combination of fresh or canned fruit.

Texas Grapefruit Parfait

½ cup **TEXAS RUBY RED Grapefruit Juice**
1 envelope unflavored gelatin
½ cup **IMPERIAL Brown Sugar**
2 cups light cream (half-and-half)
1 to 2 teaspoons lemon juice, according to taste
2 egg whites
2 tablespoons **IMPERIAL Brown Sugar**
4 **TEXAS RUBY RED Grapefruits**

Cut grapefruit in halves and section. Set sections aside and let drain. Squeeze grapefruit halves for juice. Combine grapefruit juice and gelatin in small saucepan and stir; let stand 1 minute. Warm over low heat just until gelatin is dissolved; add ½ cup **IMPERIAL Brown Sugar** and stir to dissolve sugar. Stir in cream and lemon juice and transfer to large mixing bowl. Chill thoroughly (about 1½ to 2 hours); while chilling stir occasionally, until mixture begins to thicken. Meanwhile, in medium bowl, beat egg whites to soft peak stage; gradually add the 2 tablespoons **IMPERIAL Brown Sugar** and beat until stiff peaks form. Fold into chilled mixture. Transfer to chilled parfait or wine glasses alternately with grapefruit sections. Chill until serving time.
Makes eight, 6-oz. servings

Favorite recipe from the **Texas Citrus Industry**

Amaretto di Galliano

Strawberries Amaretto

1 quart strawberries, washed and hulled
AMARETTO di GALLIANO™
1 cup finely granulated sugar

Divide berries between 4 dessert dishes. Sprinkle each serving of berries with about 1 oz. **AMARETTO di GALLIANO**™. Provide a small cup of finely granulated sugar with each dish for dipping berries.   *Serves 4*

ᵀᴴᴱ CHRISTIAN BROTHERS®

Macedonia di Frutta

1 ripe pineapple, cut into chunks
1 (16 oz.) package frozen cherries or other berries
¾ lb. green and/or red grapes
1 lb. fresh fruits in season (such as peaches, plums, nectarines) or frozen mixed fruit, sliced
1 cup **THE CHRISTIAN BROTHERS®** Napa Rosé or Chablis
¼ cup apple jelly

In a large shallow bowl, combine fruit with rosé or chablis. Chill 4 hours, turning fruit once or twice. Melt jelly in saucepan; brush over fruit to glaze.   *Makes 4 to 6 servings*

Virginia Dare's Pineapple Riviera

Place a scoop of vanilla ice cream on a slice of canned, drained pineapple. Then pour on **VIRGINIA DARE Melba** or **Strawberry-Raspberry Sauce** to cover fruit and ice cream. A fast and fancy dessert.

NABISCO BRANDS ᴵᴺᴄ

Fruit Kabobs

1 (8-ounce) can **DROMEDARY Date Nut roll**
4 large fresh or canned peach halves, each cut into 3 pieces
2 all-yellow bananas, cut into 12 (1-inch) slices
2 tablespoons butter or margarine, melted
2 tablespoons lemon juice
2 tablespoons granulated sugar
Ground cinnamon
½ cup dairy sour cream
2 tablespoons orange juice
1 teaspoon grated orange rind

Cut **DROMEDARY Date Nut Roll** crosswise into 3 pieces; then cut each piece into quarters. Thread alternately with fruit on 6

(about 7-inch) skewers. Brush nut roll pieces on all sides with butter or margarine. Brush fruit with lemon juice; then sprinkle with 1 tablespoon sugar and cinnamon. Grill or broil about 10 minutes, or until lightly browned, turning occasionally. Meanwhile, stir together next three ingredients and remaining sugar. Serve with kabobs.

Makes 6 (about 7-inch) kabobs and ⅔ cup sauce

Baked Peach Meringue
(Low Calorie/Low Sodium)

1-16 oz. can water or juice packed peach halves
6 tsp. **DIA-MEL Grape Jelly**
1 egg white
⅛ tsp. cream of tartar
2 Tbsp. **ESTEE® Granulated Fructose**

Preheat oven to 350°F. Drain juice from peaches. Arrange 6 peach halves, cut side up, in ungreased square baking pan. Fill each peach half with 1 tsp. of **DIA-MEL Grape Jelly**. To prepare meringue, beat egg white and cream of tartar in small bowl until frothy. Slowly add **ESTEE® Fructose** and continue beating until soft peaks form. Cover each peach half with meringue. Bake for 20 minutes or until tops are lightly browned.

Makes 6 servings, 1 peach half per serving

NUTRITION INFORMATION

Calories	Carbohydrates	Protein	Sodium
40	10g	1g	9mg

DIABETIC EXCHANGE INFORMATION
Fruit
1

Lite Melon Meringue

2 small honeydews or cantaloupes
4 egg whites
2 tsp. sugar
2 cups plain yogurt or ice milk
1 can (16 oz.) **DEL MONTE Lite Sliced Peaches** or **Sliced Pears**, drained

Cut melons in half. Seed. Whip egg whites with sugar until stiff. Fill melon halves with yogurt and place peach slices on top edge in pinwheel fashion. Top with meringue. Bake at 450°F., 2 to 3 minutes, until lightly browned.   *4 servings*

Lite Fruit Whip

2 cans (16 oz. each) **DEL MONTE Lite Fruit Cocktail** or **Chunky Mixed Fruits**
1 cup **DEL MONTE Unsweetened Orange Juice**, chilled
1 pkg. (3 oz.) orange or lemon-flavored gelatin
Rind of one lemon, grated
Juice of one lemon
1 tsp. vanilla extract
2 egg whites, room temperature

Drain fruit reserving ⅔ cup liquid. Add ½ cup orange juice to reserved liquid; heat to boiling. Add gelatin; dissolve completely. Stir in remaining orange juice, lemon rind, lemon juice and vanilla. Chill until slightly thickened. Add egg whites and beat with electric mixer until double in size and creamy (8 to 10 minutes). In serving bowl, spread half the fruit. Top with gelatin mixture; chill until firm. Top with remaining fruit and serve.

6 to 8 servings

Fruit Bavarian

1 package (3 oz.) flavored gelatin (use 6 oz. for heavy fruit)*
4 tablespoons sugar
1 cup boiling water
1 cup cold fruit juice
2 cups fresh, frozen, or canned fruit (Do not use fresh or frozen pineapple or kiwi fruit.)
⅔ cup **MILNOT®**, whipped

Dissolve gelatin and sugar in boiling water, add cold juice, and chill until it is slightly thickened. Beat until fluffy; add fruit. Fold stiffly whipped **MILNOT®** into fruit mixture. Pour into prepared mold (approx. 6 cups). Chill several hours or overnight until well set.

Yield: approx. 9 servings

*Note: Strawberry or raspberry especially good.

Blueberry Cobbler

1 qt. fresh or dry-pack frozen blueberries, rinsed and drained
½ cup granulated sugar
1 tablespoon cornstarch
½ teaspoon grated lemon peel
1 teaspoon lemon juice
¼ teaspoon **ANGOSTURA® Aromatic Bitters**
¼ teaspoon cinnamon
1 cup unsifted all-purpose flour
1 tablespoon granulated sugar
1½ teaspoons baking powder
2 teaspoons grated orange rind
¼ teaspoon salt
3 tablespoons shortening
⅓ cup milk
1 egg

In medium saucepan combine blueberries, ½ cup sugar, cornstarch, lemon peel, lemon juice, **ANGOSTURA® Bitters** and cinnamon. Cook over medium heat, stirring constantly, until mixture just starts to bubble. Lower heat and simmer about 5 minutes or until mixture has thickened, stirring frequently. In mixing bowl thoroughly combine flour, sugar, baking powder, orange rind and salt. Cut in shortening until mixture resembles coarse crumbs. In small bowl combine milk and egg. Beat slightly to combine. Pour all at once into flour mixture and stir just until all flour is moistened. Transfer hot blueberries to 2-quart baking dish. Drop heaping tablespoons of biscuit dough into fruit. Bake at 400° F. 20 to 25 minutes or until biscuits are browned. Serve with whipped cream or ice cream, if desired.

Yield: 4 to 6 servings

Cherry Cobbler

1 can (16 oz) red sour cherries packed in water
½ cup sugar
1 tablespoon corn starch
1 tablespoon **MAZOLA®/NUCOA® Margarine**
1 teaspoon lemon juice
3 drops red food coloring
1 recipe Biscuit Dough*

Drain cherries reserving ¾ cup juice. In small saucepan mix together juice, sugar and corn starch. Cook over medium heat stirring constantly until mixture comes to a boil and boils 1 minute. Stir in margarine, lemon juice and food coloring. Remove from heat. Add cherries. Pour hot cherry mixture into 10″ × 6″ × 2″ baking dish. Drop Biscuit Dough by teaspoonfuls onto hot cherry mixture. Bake in 400°F oven 20 to 30 minutes or until Biscuit Dough is golden. *Makes 6 servings*

*Biscuit Dough

1 cup unsifted flour
1 tablespoon sugar
2 teaspoons baking powder
¼ teaspoon salt
¼ teaspoon nutmeg
¼ cup **MAZOLA® Corn Oil**
⅓ cup milk

Stir together flour, sugar, baking powder, salt and nutmeg. Stir in corn oil. Add milk and mix well.

Spicy Pear Cobbler

2 Tbsp. cornstarch
½ tsp. nutmeg
2-16 oz. cans **S&W® Natural Style Bartlett Pears**, drained (reserve juice)
½ cup **S&W® Seedless Raisins**
½ cup **S&W® Shelled Walnuts**, chopped
1 Tbsp. butter
1½ cups all-purpose flour
3 Tbsp. sugar
2 tsp. baking powder
¼ tsp. salt
6 Tbsp. butter
¾ cup milk
1 egg, beaten

Combine cornstarch and nutmeg; blend in the reserved juice using a wire whip to eliminate any lumps. Cook over medium heat until thick and bubbly. Remove from heat. Stir in pears, raisins, walnuts and butter. Turn hot pear mixture into 7 x 11″ baking pan. Meanwhile, prepare topping by sifting together flour, sugar, baking powder and salt. Cut in butter until mixture resembles coarse crumbs. Combine milk with beaten egg. Add to dry mixture and stir just to moisten. Spoon on pear mixture in 8 portions. Bake at 400° for 20-25 minutes or until top is golden brown. Serve with cream or ice cream. *Serves 8*

Since 1882
Breakstone's®

Ginger Cream Dip

1 cup **BREAKSTONE'S® Sour Cream**
2 tablespoons honey
½ teaspoon grated orange rind
⅛ teaspoon ground ginger

Combine ingredients; mix well. Chill. Serve with fruit.   *1 cup*

Cakes

Double Chocolate Cheesecake

Crust:
¼ cup butter or margarine
25 **OREO Chocolate Sandwich Cookies**, crushed

Filling:
2 (8-ounce) packages cream cheese, at room temperature
6 eggs, separated, at room temperature
4 (1-ounce) squares semi-sweet chocolate, melted
2 teaspoons vanilla extract
½ cup sugar

Decoration:
1 (1-ounce) square semi-sweet chocolate
Chocolate curls

1. **MAKE CRUST:**
In medium saucepan, over low heat, melt butter or margarine; remove from heat; stir in **OREO** crumbs. Press evenly onto bottom and sides of 9-inch spring-form pan; refrigerate while preparing filling.

2. **MAKE FILLING:**
In large bowl, with electric mixer at medium speed, beat cream cheese until light and fluffy; beat in egg yolks, melted chocolate and vanilla extract until smooth, about 3 minutes; set aside.

3. In another large bowl, with electric mixer at high speed, beat egg whites until soft peaks form; gradually add sugar, beating until stiff peaks form. Using rubber spatula, gently fold beaten egg whites, ⅓ at a time, into cream cheese mixture. Pour into crust; freeze 4 hours.

4. **MAKE CHOCOLATE LOOP DECORATION:**
In small saucepan, over low heat, melt 1 (1-ounce) square semi-sweet chocolate; remove from heat; let cool to room temperature.

5. On 11×8½-inch sheet of white paper, draw 1 (6-inch) circle; on outside of circle, draw 12 (1-inch) circles, spaced evenly around circle. Place on cookie sheet; cover with wax paper, securing wax paper edges under cookie sheet.

6. Using No. 1 decorating tip, pipe melted chocolate onto wax paper over outline (or drizzle chocolate, a little at a time, from teaspoon); freeze until firm, about 30 minutes.   *(Continued)*

7. **TO SERVE:**
Remove sides of pan; carefully remove wax paper from Chocolate Loop Decoration; set on frozen cheesecake. Garnish with chocolate curls.   *Makes 10 to 12 servings*

Individual Cheesecakes

8 **NILLA Wafers**
2 (3-ounce) packages cream cheese, softened
⅓ cup **SNACK MATE Sharp Cheddar Pasteurized Process Cheese Spread**
2 eggs
½ cup granulated sugar
1 teaspoon lemon juice
1 (20-ounce) can blueberry or cherry pie filling

1. Preheat oven to 350°F. Line 8 (2½-inch) cupcake pans or muffin tins with paper liners. Place one **NILLA Wafer** in bottom of each.
2. In medium bowl, with electric mixer at medium speed, beat together cream cheese and **SNACK MATE Cheese** 2 minutes. Add eggs, sugar and lemon juice; beat an additional 3 minutes. (Mixture will not be smooth.)
3. Fill each cupcake liner with ¼-cup cheesecake mixture. Bake 30 minutes; place on wire rack to cool completely. Top each cheesecake with a little blueberry or cherry pie filling; refrigerate additional pie filling for later use.

Makes 8 individual cheesecakes

MICROWAVE METHOD:
1. Line 9 (6-ounce) microwave-proof custard cups with a double layer of paper liners. Proceed as in Steps 1 and 2.
2. Fill each cup with a scant ¼-cup cheesecake mixture. Arrange filled cups in a circle in microwave oven. Microwave at 100% power 5 to 6 minutes, re-arranging position of cups after 2 minutes. Cool and top with pie filling as in Step 3.

Sour Cream Lemon Cheesecake

1 package **DUNCAN HINES® Pudding Recipe Lemon Cake Mix**
3 eggs
2 tablespoons flour
1 tablespoon plus 1 teaspoon **CRISCO® Oil** or **PURITAN® Oil**
2 cartons (8 ounces each) dairy sour cream
½ cup sugar
1 teaspoon lemon juice
1 cup milk
2 drops yellow food coloring
1 can (21 ounces) blueberry pie filling

Preheat oven to 300°. Measure out 1½ cups dry cake mix; set aside. Stir together remaining dry cake mix, 1 egg, flour, and oil in large bowl. Press this crumb mixture evenly into bottom and three-quarters of the way up the sides of a 13×9×2-inch pan.

In same bowl, blend sour cream, sugar, 2 eggs, reserved cake mix, and lemon juice 1 minute at low speed. Gradually add milk and food coloring while beating 2 minutes at medium speed. Pour into crumb crust. Bake at 300° for 45 to 50 minutes, or until center is firm. Do not overbake. Cool at room temperature 1 hour. Top with blueberry pie filling or your favorite pie filling and refrigerate. *One 13 × 9-inch cake*

Granny Apple Cheesecake

Crust:
1¼ cups graham cracker crumbs
¼ cup butter or margarine, melted
2 tablespoons sugar
¼ teaspoon ground cinnamon

Apple-Cheese Filling:
2 envelopes unflavored gelatine
¾ cup sugar, divided
1 cup low-fat milk
2 eggs, separated
1 tablespoon lemon juice
½ teaspoon grated lemon peel
¼ teaspoon salt
2 cups (1 pound) small curd cottage cheese
2 large **CAPE GRANNY SMITH Apples**, pared, cored and shredded (2 cups)

CRUST:
In small bowl, combine graham cracker crumbs, butter, sugar and cinnamon; mix well. Press firmly into a 9-inch spring-form pan, covering bottom and 1¼ inches up sides. Chill 1 hour.

APPLE-CHEESE FILLING:
In medium saucepan, combine gelatine with ½ cup sugar. Stir in milk, egg yolks, lemon juice, lemon peel and salt. Cook over low heat, stirring constantly with wire whisk, until gelatine dissolves. Remove from heat. In large bowl beat cottage cheese until smooth. Gradually beat in gelatine mixture. Stir in shredded apples. Chill, stirring occasionally, until mixture mounds slightly when dropped from a spoon. In small bowl, beat egg whites until foamy. Gradually add remaining ¼ cup sugar, beating until stiff peaks form. Fold into apple-cheese mixture. Pour into prepared cake pan. Chill overnight or 8 to 12 hours until firm. *Yield: 12 servings*

Campbell's

Regal Cheesecake Pie

Crumb Crust:
2 cups fine vanilla wafer or graham cracker crumbs
6 tablespoons butter or margarine, melted
¼ cup sugar

Filling:
12 ounces cream cheese, softened
⅔ cup sugar
3 eggs
1 can (11 ounces) **CAMPBELL'S Condensed Cheddar Cheese Soup**
2 tablespoons lemon juice
1 teaspoon grated lemon rind
1 teaspoon vanilla extract
¼ teaspoon almond extract

Topping:
1 cup sour cream
¼ cup sugar
1 teaspoon grated lemon rind
1 teaspoon vanilla extract

TO MAKE CRUST:
Combine crumbs, butter and sugar. Press firmly into 10-inch pie plate. Chill for 1 hour.

TO MAKE FILLING:
In mixing bowl, blend cream cheese until smooth. With medium speed of electric mixer, blend sugar and eggs alternately into cream cheese. Blend in *1 cup* soup. Stir in lemon juice, rind and flavorings. Pour into chilled piecrust. Bake at 350°F. for 50 minutes. Meanwhile, for topping, blend remaining soup with sour cream, sugar, lemon rind and vanilla. Spread on pie. Bake 5 minutes more. Cool; chill. Garnish chilled cheesecake with the following fruit topping*

*Golden Peach Surprise

Drain 1 can (about 16 ounces) sliced cling peaches, reserving 2 tablespoons syrup. Arrange peaches on cheesecake pie. In saucepan, combine reserved syrup, 2 teaspoons cornstarch, ½ cup peach preserves and ⅛ teaspoon almond extract. Cook over low heat, stirring until thickened. Cool. Spoon on cheesecake; chill.

Kahlúa® Cheesecake

Zwieback Crust*
2 envelopes unflavored gelatin
½ cup **KAHLÚA®** liqueur
½ cup water
3 eggs, separated
¼ cup sugar
⅛ tsp. salt
2 (8 oz.) packages cream cheese
1 cup whipping cream
Shaved or curled semi-sweet chocolate

Prepare Zwieback Crust. In top of double boiler, soften gelatin in **KAHLÚA®** and water. Beat in egg yolks, sugar and salt. Cook over boiling water, stirring constantly, until slightly thickened. Beat cheese until fluffy. Gradually beat in **KAHLÚA®** mixture; cool. Beat egg whites until stiff but not dry. Beat cream stiff. Fold egg whites and cream into cheese mixture. Pour into prepared pan. Chill 4 or 5 hours, or overnight. Remove from refrigerator 15 minutes before serving. Decorate with shaved or curled chocolate. (To add flavor, spoon a little **KAHLÚA®** over each serving.) *Makes 12 servings*

*Zwieback Crust

Blend 1½ cups fine Zwieback crumbs, and ⅓ cup **each** sugar and melted butter together. Press firmly over bottom and half way up sides of a 9-inch springform pan. Bake in a moderate oven (350 degrees F) 8 to 10 minutes. Cool.

KITCHENS OF
Sara Lee

Fruit Topped Cheese Cakes

6 frozen **SARA LEE Individual Cheese Danish**
½ cup cherry or blueberry pie filling

Warm Danish according to package directions. Place Danish on plates. Spoon about 1 tablespoon pie filling on each Danish.
Makes 6 servings

Heavenly Heart Chocolate Cake

¾ cup HERSHEY'S® Unsweetened Cocoa
⅔ cup boiling water
¾ cup butter or margarine, softened
2 cups sugar
1 teaspoon vanilla
2 eggs
2 cups unsifted cake flour or 1¾ cups all-purpose flour
1¼ teaspoons baking soda
¼ teaspoon salt
¾ cup buttermilk or sour milk*

Stir together cocoa and boiling water in small bowl until smooth; set aside. Cream butter or margarine, sugar and vanilla in large mixer bowl until fluffy; beat in eggs and cocoa mixture. Combine flour, baking soda and salt; add alternately with buttermilk or sour milk to creamed mixture. Pour batter into two greased and floured heart-shaped pans or two 9-inch layer pans. Bake at 350° for 30 to 35 minutes or until cake tester inserted in center comes out clean. Cool 10 minutes; remove from pans. Cool completely; frost with Glossy Chocolate Sour Cream Frosting and pipe with Creamy Buttercream Frosting. Sprinkle with chopped nuts, if desired.

*To Sour Milk: Use 2 teaspoons vinegar plus milk to equal ¾ cup.

Glossy Chocolate Sour Cream Frosting

1½ cups HERSHEY'S® Semi-Sweet Chocolate Mini Chips
¾ cup sour cream
2 cups confectioners' sugar
1 teaspoon vanilla

Melt Mini Chips in top of double boiler over hot water. Stir constantly until completely melted. Remove from heat, beat in sour cream, confectioners' sugar and vanilla.

About 2½ cups frosting

Creamy Buttercream Frosting

2 cups confectioners' sugar
¼ cup butter or margarine
2½ tablespoons milk
½ teaspoon vanilla

Combine ingredients until smooth and creamy in a small bowl. With decorating tube, pipe frosting around edges of cake.

About 1 cup frosting

Black Forest Cherry Cake

1 18.5-ounce pkg. chocolate cake mix (do not use cake mix with pudding added)
2 21-ounce cans THANK YOU® BRAND Cherry Pie Filling
¼ cup oil
3 eggs

Grease and flour a 12-cup Bundt® pan. Preheat oven to 350°. Combine cake mix, 1 can of pie filling, oil and eggs; beat well with mixer until batter is smooth. Pour in prepared pan. Bake 45-50 minutes or until cake springs back from light touch. Cool in pan 25 minutes, invert onto rack to finish cooling. Decorate and serve with one 21-ounce can Cherry Pie Filling and whipped cream.

Chocolate Peanut Ripple Cake

Cake:
1 pkg. PILLSBURY PLUS Fudge Marble Cake Mix
1 cup dairy sour cream
½ cup creamy peanut butter
¼ cup water
3 eggs
½ cup chopped peanuts

Frosting:
1 can PILLSBURY Ready To Spread Chocolate Fudge Frosting Supreme
2 tablespoons creamy peanut butter
1 tablespoon chopped peanuts

Heat oven to 350°F. Grease and flour two 8 or 9-inch round cake pans. In large bowl, blend cake mix (reserve marble pouch), sour cream, ½ cup peanut butter, water and eggs until moistened. Beat 2 minutes at highest speed. Fold in ½ cup chopped peanuts. Pour three-fourths of batter into prepared pans.

To the remaining batter add marble pouch and 2 tablespoons water; blend well. Spoon randomly over yellow batter. Swirl with spoon in a folding motion, turning pan while folding.

Bake at 350°F. for 35 to 45 minutes or until toothpick inserted in center comes out clean. Cool in pans 15 minutes; then remove. Cool completely.

Blend frosting with 2 tablespoons peanut butter. Spread small amount (about ⅓ cup) between cake layers. Frost sides and top with remaining frosting. Garnish with 1 tablespoon chopped peanuts.

12 servings

HIGH ALTITUDE—Above 3500 Feet: Add 3 tablespoons flour to dry cake mix. Bake at 375°F. for 30 to 35 minutes.

German Sweet Chocolate Cake

1 package (4 oz.) BAKER'S® GERMAN'S® Sweet Chocolate
⅓ cup boiling water
2 cups sifted SWANS DOWN® Cake Flour
¾ teaspoon baking soda
¼ teaspoon salt
¾ cup butter or margarine
1⅓ cups sugar
3 egg yolks
¾ teaspoon vanilla
¾ cup buttermilk
3 egg whites, stiffly beaten
Coconut-Pecan Filling and Frosting*

Melt chocolate in boiling water. Cool. Sift flour with soda and salt. Cream butter. Gradually beat in sugar and continue beating until light and fluffy. Add egg yolks, one at a time, beating after each. Blend in vanilla and chocolate; mix until blended. Add flour mixture alternately with buttermilk, beating after each addition until smooth. Fold in egg whites.

Pour into two 9-inch layer pans which have been lined on bottoms with paper. Bake at 350° for about 30 minutes, or until cake springs back when lightly pressed in center. Cool in pans 15 minutes. Then remove from pans and finish cooling on racks. Spread Coconut-Pecan Filling and Frosting between layers and over top of cake.

*Coconut-Pecan Filling and Frosting

Combine 1 can (5.33 oz.) evaporated milk, ⅔ cup sugar, 2 egg yolks, slightly beaten, ⅓ cup butter or margarine and ¾ teaspoon vanilla in saucepan. Cook and stir over medium heat until mixture thickens, about 10 minutes. Remove from heat; add 1 cup **BAKER'S® ANGEL FLAKE® Coconut** and ⅔ cup chopped pecans. Beat until cool and of spreading consistency.

Makes about 2 cups

Chocolate Cake Roll With Almond-Plum Filling

4 eggs, separated, at room temperature
¾ cup granulated sugar
1 teaspoon vanilla extract
¾ cup sifted cake flour
3 tablespoons unsweetened cocoa
1 tablespoon instant coffee powder
¾ teaspoon baking powder
¼ teaspoon salt
Sifted powdered sugar
Almond-Plum Filling*
½ cup **BLUE DIAMOND® Sliced Natural Almonds,** toasted
¼ cup plum jam

Grease 15 ×10×1-inch jelly roll pan; line with waxed paper; lightly grease waxed paper. In small bowl beat egg yolks with electric mixer until thick and lemon-colored, 3 to 5 minutes; gradually add ½ cup of the sugar, beating until pale yellow. Blend in vanilla; set aside. In large bowl, beat egg whites to soft peaks; gradually add remaining ¼ cup sugar, beating to stiff peaks. Fold yolk mixture into whites. Sift together flour, cocoa, coffee powder, baking powder and salt; fold into egg mixture. Spread in prepared jelly roll pan.

Bake in a 375 degree F. oven for 12 to 15 minutes or just until surface springs back when gently pressed with fingertip. Immediately turn out onto towel generously dusted with powdered sugar; peel away waxed paper. Roll up starting with narrow end; cool. Unroll; spread with Almond-Plum Filling; sprinkle with almonds and reroll. In small saucepan, melt ¼ cup plum jam. Brush on cake roll. Garnish with additional almonds if desired.

Makes 10 servings

*Almond-Plum Filling

Thoroughly blend 1 to 1⅓ cups Almond Paste (recipe follows) and ¾ cup plum jam.

(Continued)

**Home-Made Almond Paste

1½ cups **BLUE DIAMOND® Blanched Whole Almonds**
1½ cups sifted powdered sugar
1 egg white
1 teaspoon almond extract
¼ teaspoon salt

Grind almonds, a portion at a time, in electric blender or food chopper using fine blade. Combine with remaining ingredients and work to a stiff paste. Store in airtight container or disposable plastic bag.   *This makes 13 ounces (1⅓ cups) almond paste*

Best Foods®
HELLMANN'S®

Chocolate Mayonnaise Cake

2 cups unsifted flour
⅔ cup unsweetened cocoa
1¼ teaspoons baking soda
¼ teaspoon baking powder
1⅔ cups sugar
3 eggs
1 teaspoon vanilla
1 cup **BEST FOODS®/HELLMANN'S® Real Mayonnaise**
1⅓ cups water

Grease and flour bottoms of 2 (9 × 1½-inch) round baking pans. In medium bowl stir together flour, cocoa, baking soda and baking powder; set aside. In large bowl with mixer at high speed beat sugar, eggs and vanilla, occasionally scraping bowl, 3 minutes or until light and fluffy. Reduce speed to low; beat in **Real Mayonnaise**. Add flour mixture in 4 additions alternately with water, beginning and ending with flour. Pour into prepared pans. Bake in 350°F oven 30 to 35 minutes or until cake tester inserted in center comes out clean. Cool in pans 10 minutes. Remove; cool on wire racks. Frost as desired. Garnish with sliced almonds.

Makes 2 (9-inch) layers

Ever-So-Easy Fruitcake

2½ cups unsifted flour
1 teaspoon baking soda
2 eggs, slightly beaten
1 (28-ounce) jar **NONE SUCH® Ready-to-Use Mince Meat**
1 (14-ounce) can **EAGLE® Brand Sweetened Condensed Milk** (NOT evaporated milk)
2 cups (1 pound) mixed candied fruit
1 cup coarsely chopped nuts

Preheat oven to 350°F. Grease a 9-inch tube pan; line with wax paper and grease again (or use generously greased and floured 10-inch fluted tube pan). Sift together flour and baking soda; set aside. In large bowl, combine remaining ingredients; blend in dry ingredients. Pour into prepared pan. Bake 1 hour and 50 minutes or until toothpick inserted near center comes out clean. Cool 15 minutes. Turn out of pan; remove wax paper. Garnish as desired.

Makes one 9-inch cake

Orange Cake

¾ cup shortening
1¼ cups sugar
8 egg yolks
1 orange, juice and grated rind
2½ cups E-Z-BAKE Flour
½ teaspoon salt
3 teaspoons baking powder
¾ cup milk

HAND-MIXING METHOD:
Cream shortening and sugar until fluffy. Beat yolks until thick and lemon colored. Add to creamed mixture and beat smooth. Then add orange juice and rind. Add sifted dry ingredients alternately with milk. Beat thoroughly. Bake in a greased and floured pan in moderate oven (350° F.) 50 to 60 minutes. After baking, let cake stand a few minutes before removing from pan.

ELECTRIC-MIXER METHOD:
Measure shortening into bowl. Add flour, resifted with sugar, salt, leavening and three-fourths of the milk. Beat 2 minutes at low to medium speed, frequently scraping down sides of bowl and beater. Add unbeaten eggs, remaining milk and flavoring, and beat another 2 minutes. For best results, have all ingredients at room temperature.

Yellow Icing

2 cups sugar
½ cup water
¼ cup white corn syrup
4 egg yolks
¼ teaspoon salt
1 teaspoon lemon juice
½ teaspoon orange rind
1 teaspoon orange juice
2 tablespoons cream
½ cup coconut

Cook sugar, water and corn syrup until mixture spins long double threads. Beat yolks until thick and lemon colored. Add salt and pour syrup over eggs in continuous stream, beating continuously until cool and fudgelike. Add cream, fruit juices and orange rind. Frost cake. If icing gets too stiff, thin with a little sweet cream. Sprinkle with coconut before frosting sets.

Orange Chiffon Layer Cake

2 egg whites
⅓ cup sugar
2 cups sifted cake flour
1 cup sugar
3 teaspoons baking powder
1 teaspoon salt
½ cup orange juice
½ cup skim milk
½ cup PURITAN® Oil
2 egg yolks

Preheat oven to 350°.

In a small bowl beat egg whites with ⅓ cup sugar until thick and glossy but not stiff. Set aside. Combine flour, 1 cup sugar, baking powder and salt in a large mixing bowl. Add orange juice, milk, **PURITAN® Oil**, and egg yolks. Mix at medium speed for 3 minutes; scrape bottom and sides of bowl often. Fold egg whites into batter until well-blended. Pour into two greased and floured 8 × 1½-inch layer pans. Bake at 350° for 25 to 30 minutes until center springs back when touched lightly. Cool 10 to 20 minutes, then remove from pans. *Makes two 8-inch layers*

General Mills

Orange Chiffon Cake

2¼ cups SOFTASILK® Cake Flour or 2 cups GOLD MEDAL® All-Purpose Flour*
1½ cups sugar
3 teaspoons baking powder
1 teaspoon salt
½ cup vegetable oil
5 egg yolks (with SOFTASILK® Flour) or 7 egg yolks (with GOLD MEDAL® Flour)
¾ cup cold water
2 tablespoons grated orange peel
1 cup egg whites (7 or 8)
½ teaspoon cream of tartar
Orange or Lemon Butter Frosting (recipe follows)

Heat oven to 325°. Mix flour, sugar, baking powder and salt in bowl. Make a well and add in order: oil, egg yolks, water and orange peel. Beat with spoon until smooth. Beat egg whites and cream of tartar in large bowl on high speed until stiff peaks form. Pour egg yolk mixture gradually over beaten whites, gently folding with rubber spatula just until blended. Pour into ungreased tube pan, 10x4 inches. Bake until top springs back when touched lightly, about 1¼ hours. Invert pan on heatproof funnel; let hang until cake is cold. Frost with Orange or Lemon Butter Frosting.

*If using self-rising flour, omit baking powder and salt.

Orange or Lemon Butter Frosting

⅓ cup margarine or butter, softened
3 cups powdered sugar
1 tablespoon plus 2 teaspoons grated orange or lemon peel
About 3 tablespoons orange or lemon juice

Beat all ingredients until of spreading consistency.

Featherweight®

Applesauce Cake

1 cup FEATHERWEIGHT® Corn Flour
¾ cup sugar
¾ tsp. baking soda
¾ tsp. salt
¼ tsp. each cinnamon, nutmeg, cloves, allspice
¼ cup shortening
¾ cup FEATHERWEIGHT® Applesauce
1 egg

Sift dry ingredients together and place in mixing bowl. Add shortening and one half of the applesauce and mix well. Add remainder of applesauce and egg and mix well. Pour batter into greased cake pan (approx. 8″ × 8″). Bake at 350°F. for 35 minutes.

VARIATIONS:

Fold in ⅓ cup each of chopped dates, raisins, and nuts. Sprinkle with topping of ¼ cup nuts and one tablespoon sugar.

Apple Pie Cake

1 pkg. spice cake mix
2 cans LUCKY LEAF® Apple Pie Filling
2 Tbsp. lemon juice, plus enough LUCKY LEAF® Apple Juice to make 1 cup liquid or 1 cup water

Sprinkle ½ box cake mix into greased oblong 13″ × 9″ baking dish. Pour on 2 cans LUCKY LEAF® Apple Pie Filling, then remaining cake mix. Mix apple juice and lemon juice and carefully distribute over top. Bake at 350° for 1 hour.

Makes 10 servings

Mother's Day Date Dessert

Date-Nut Loaf:
2 Tbsp. butter
½ cup honey
1 egg
1 tsp. grated lemon peel
2 tsp. lemon juice
1½ cups unbleached white flour
¼ tsp. salt
⅛ tsp. baking soda
1 tsp. baking powder
½ cup buttermilk
1 cup chopped pitted SUN WORLD® Dates
½ cup chopped walnuts

Banana Topping:
1 egg
2 Tbsp. sugar
2 Tbsp. skim milk
1 tsp. lemon juice
½ chopped banana
1 cup whipped low-calorie dessert topping

Preheat oven to 350 degrees. Cream the butter and slowly beat in the honey. Beat in the egg, lemon peel and lemon juice. Combine the flour, salt, baking soda and baking powder and add alternately with the buttermilk to the batter. Fold in the dates and walnuts. Pour the mixture into a greased 9 × 5 × 3 inch pan. Bake 50 to 60 minutes or until done.

Cool the date-nut loaf and top with the following: In small saucepan beat egg, sugar and milk. Cook and stir over low heat until mixture thickens slightly. Add lemon juice while stirring. Cool thoroughly. Add chopped bananas and fold in whipped topping. Chill and serve as topping for date-nut loaf.

Sunlite® Carrot Cake

1½ cups SUNLITE® Oil
2 cups sugar
3 eggs
2 tsp. vanilla
2 cups all-purpose flour
2 tsp. cinnamon
2 tsp. baking soda
1 tsp. salt
1 (7-oz.) pkg. flake coconut
2 cups shredded carrots
1 (13½-oz.) can crushed pineapple, drained
1 cup chopped nuts

In a large bowl, thoroughly combine SUNLITE® Oil, sugar, eggs and vanilla. Sift together flour, cinnamon, baking soda, and salt; add to first mixture and mix well. Stir in coconut, shredded carrots, pineapple and nuts. Pour into greased and floured 13 × 9 × 2-inch pan. Bake at 350° 50 to 60 minutes until center of cake is firm to the touch. Cool in pan. Frost as desired.

Makes 15 servings

Golden Beauty Prune Cake

1 cup snipped cooked SUNSWEET® Prunes
½ cup butter or margarine
1 cup granulated sugar
½ cup brown sugar, packed
1 teaspoon vanilla
2 large eggs, beaten
2½ cups sifted all-purpose flour
¾ teaspoon baking powder
¾ teaspoon soda
¾ teaspoon salt
½ teaspoon cinnamon
¼ teaspoon nutmeg
¼ teaspoon cloves
1 cup buttermilk
Mocha Frosting*

Cook prunes by package directions; drain and snip. Cream butter with sugars and vanilla until light and fluffy. Beat in eggs. (Mixture may appear slightly curdled.) Resift flour with baking powder, soda, salt and spices. Blend into creamed mixture alternately with buttermilk, beginning and ending with flour mixture. Fold in prunes. Turn into two well greased, 8-inch layer cake pans. Bake in oven center at 375°F. for about 30 minutes, until cakes test done. Remove from oven; let stand 10 minutes, then turn out onto wire racks to cool. When cold, spread Mocha Frosting between layers and on top and sides of cake.   *Makes one 8-inch cake*

Mocha Frosting

Dissolve 1 teaspoon instant coffee powder in ¼ cup milk. Combine with ⅓ cup soft butter or margarine, and 1 pound powdered sugar, sifted. Beat until smooth, adding a few drops more milk if needed for good spreading consistency.

31

Amaretto Raisin Bundt® Cake

1 pkg. **PILLSBURY Pound Cake Supreme BUNDT®
   Cake Mix**
½ dairy sour cream
¼ cup margarine or butter, softened
½ cup water
⅓ cup **HIRAM WALKER Amaretto** liqueur
3 eggs
2 cups (1 lb.) candied fruit mixture
1 cup **SUN-MAID® Raisins**
1 cup chopped nuts

Sauce:
1½ cups sugar
4 tablespoons cornstarch
1½ cups water
4 tablespoons margarine or butter
¼ cup **HIRAM WALKER Amaretto** liqueur
2 tablespoons lemon juice
½ cup **SUN-MAID® Raisins**

Heat oven to 325°F. Grease 12-cup **Bundt®** pan. In large bowl, combine two clear packets of cake mix and remaining cake ingredients except fruit, raisins, and nuts. Blend until moistened; beat 2 minutes at medium speed. Fold in fruit, raisins and nuts. Pour into pan. Bake at 325°F. for 70 to 80 minutes until toothpick inserted in center comes out clean. Cool upright in pan on rack 25 minutes; invert onto plate. Cool completely. Sprinkle or sift topping packet over top of cake.

To prepare sauce, mix sugar and cornstarch in saucepan. Gradually stir in water. Over medium heat, stirring constantly, heat to boiling; boil 1 minute. Remove from heat; stir in margarine, Amaretto, juice and raisins. Serve warm over cooled cake.

16 servings

General Mills

Velvet Cream Cake

1 package **BETTY CROCKER®** any flavor **Creamy
   Frosting Mix**
1½ cups whipping cream
1 teaspoon vanilla
1 package **BETTY CROCKER SUPERMOIST®** any
   flavor **Cake Mix**
Glaze*
2 tablespoons finely chopped pistachio nuts or walnuts

Mix 2 cups of the frosting mix (dry), the whipping cream and vanilla in small mixer bowl; refrigerate 1 hour. Bake cake mix in 2 round pans, 9x1½ inches, as directed on package; cool. Split cake to make 4 layers. (To split, mark side of cake with wooden picks and cut with sharp pointed knife.) Beat frosting mixture on low speed until blended. Beat on high speed until soft peaks form, about 3 minutes. Fill each cake layer with 1 cup frosting mixture. Spread Glaze over top; sprinkle with nuts. Store in refrigerator.

*Glaze

Mix remaining frosting mix and 2 tablespoons boiling water. Beat on high speed until smooth, 2 to 3 minutes. If necessary, stir in 1 to 2 teaspoons additional water until of desired consistency.

California Sunshine Cake

Cake:
1½ cups **BLUE RIBBON® Finely Chopped Almonds**
1 pkg. **PILLSBURY Plus Yellow Cake Mix**
1 cup water
⅓ cup oil
1 teaspoon almond extract, if desired
3 eggs

Filling:
12-oz. pkg. (about 2 cups) pitted prunes
½ cup amaretto or orange juice

Frosting:
1½ cups whipping cream
3 tablespoons sugar
2 teaspoons amaretto or vanilla extract

Garnish:
Whole pitted prunes and **BLUE RIBBON® Whole
   Blanched Almonds**, toasted* or Amaretto Almonds**

CAKE:
Heat oven to 350° F. Grease and flour two 8 or 9-inch round cake pans. To prepare top layer of cake, sprinkle ½ cup chopped almonds in bottom of *one* prepared pan. In large bowl, blend all cake ingredients except almonds at low speed; beat 2 minutes at *highest speed.* Stir in remaining 1 cup almonds. Pour batter into prepared pans. Bake at 350° F. for 30 to 40 minutes or until toothpick inserted in center comes out clean. Cool cake in pans 15 minutes then invert layers on cooling racks. Cool completely.

FILLING:
In electric blender container, combine about half of each of the filling ingredients. Blend until almost smooth, turning blender on and off and scraping sides of container as needed. Repeat with remaining ingredients; set aside.

FROSTING:
In small bowl, whip cream until foamy. Gradually add sugar and *2 teaspoons* amaretto; continue whipping until stiff peaks form. Stir ½ cup whipped cream into prune filling. Spread prepared prune filling between cake layers, keeping almond side on top. Frost sides of cake with remaining whipped cream; garnish with prunes and almonds. Store cake loosely covered in refrigerator.

Makes 12 servings

*Toasted Almonds

Spread almonds in an ungreased baking pan or skillet. Place in a 350° F. oven or over medium-low heat on a range top for about 10 minutes, until almonds are a light golden brown; stir once or twice to assure even browning. Note that almonds will continue to brown slightly after being removed from the heat.

**Amaretto Almonds

Heat oven to 300° F. Oil one cookie sheet. In small bowl, combine *½ cup blanched whole almonds* and *4 teaspoons amaretto*; arrange in single layer on prepared pan. Bake at 300° F. for 20 to 25 minutes, tossing often, until glazed and lightly browned; cool.

HIGH ALTITUDE—Above 3500 feet: Add 3 tablespoons flour to dry cake mix. Bake at 375° F. for 25 to 35 minutes.

Chocolate Mayonnaise Cake
Best Foods®/Hellmann's® *(Best Foods, A Unit of CPC North America)*

German Sweet Bread
Blue Ribbon® *(Continental Nut Co.)*

Ever-So-Easy Fruitcake
None Such®, Eagle® Brand *(Borden Inc.)*

Pistachio Pudding Cake
Jell-O® *(General Foods Corp.)*

Peanut Butter Spice Cake
Colonial® *(Colonial Sugars, Inc.)*

Chocolate Peanut Ripple Cake
Pillsbury *(The Pillsbury Company)*

Sunlite® Carrot Cake
(Hunt-Wesson Kitchens)

Kahlúa® Cheesecake
(Maidstone Wine & Spirits)

Wheat Germ Almond Cake
Kretschmer, Robin Hood® *(International Multifoods)*

Marble Chiffon Cake *(top)*, Fudge Chiffon Pie *(center)*, Fluted Chocolate Cups *(bottom)*
Hershey's® *(Hershey Foods Corporation)*

Strawberry Spiced Shortcake, Fruit Topped Cheese Cakes,
Apple Danish à la Mode
Sara Lee *(Kitchens of Sara Lee)*

Strawberry Shortcakes
Bisquick® *(General Mills, Inc.)*

Pumpkin Pie
Milnot® *(Milnot Co.)*

Coconut Cream Pie
Calavo® *(Calavo Growers of California)*

Bits 'O Brickle® Ice Cream Pie & Sauce
Heath® *(L. S. Heath & Sons, Inc.)*

Golden Meringue Dessert Bars
Dole® *(Castle & Cooke Foods)*

Fresh Strawberry Pie
Continental *(Globe Products Co., Inc.)*

Eggnog Custard Pie
Thank You® **Brand** *(Michigan Fruit Canners)*

Fruit Glacé Pie
Keebler® *(Keebler Company)*

Joy Choy Pie
La Choy® *(La Choy Food Products)*

Apple Pie *(top)*, Apple Crescents *(bottom)*
Argo®/Kingsford's®, **Mazola®/Nucoa®** *(Best Foods, A Unit of CPC North America)*

Raspberry Paradise Pie
3-Minute Brand® *(National Oats Company Inc.)*

Colombian Fresh Banana Cake With Sea Foam Frosting
Coca-Cola® *(The Coca-Cola Company)*

Tangy Lemon Squares
Minute Maid® *(The Coca-Cola Company)*

Blueberry Cobbler
Angostura® Bitters *(North American Blueberry Council)*

Walnut Prune Soufflé
Gerber® *(Gerber Products Co.)*

Cranberry-Almond Braid *(top)*, Cherry & Nut Swirls *(bottom)*
Fleischmann's®, **Planters®** *(Nabisco Brands, Inc.)*

Simple Stollen
Pillsbury *(The Pillsbury Company)*

Grape-Glazed Steamed Pudding
Smucker's *(The J. M. Smucker Co.)*

Individual Apple-Oat Crisp
Quaker® *(Quaker Oats Company)*

Chocolate Cake Roll With Almond-Plum Filling
Blue Diamond® *(California Almond Growers Exchange)*

Baked Alaska in Patty Shells
Pepperidge Farm® *(Pepperidge Farm, Inc.)*

"Lady Be Good" Fingers
Domino® *(Amstar Corporation)*

Warm Fruitful Compote
Stokely's Finest® *(Stokely-Van Camp, Inc.)*

Royal **Courvoisier**® Poundcake *(top left)*, Orange **Courvoisier**®
Sauce *(top right)*, Frozen **Tia Maria**® Mousse Cake *(center)*,
Orange **Drambuie**® Pie *(bottom)*
(W. A. Taylor & Co.)

43

Dessert Fruit Taco
Lawry's® *(Lawry's Foods, Inc.)*

Marinated Fruit Bowl
Hiram Walker *(Hiram Walker Inc.)*

Fondue Dippers, Choco-Bar Fondue
Hershey's® *(Hershey Foods Corp.)*

Lite Fruit Whip
Del Monte *(Del Monte Corp.)*

44

Grasshopper Pie *(top)*, Mocha Mousse *(bottom)*
Arrow® *(Heublein Inc.)*

Lemon Ice
Bertolli® *(Bertolli U.S.A.)*

Apple Betty
Bran Chex® *(Ralston Purina Company)*

Chocolate Custard
Alba *(Heinz U.S.A.)*

Peach Melba Cake
Knox® *(Thomas J. Lipton, Inc.)*

Lemon-Butter Snowbars
Land O Lakes® *(Land O' Lakes, Inc.)*

Pumpkin Dandies *(left)*, Fireside Pumpkin Cookies *(top)*, Ice Cream Pumpkin Pies *(bottom)*
Libby's® *(Libby, McNeill & Libby, Inc.)*

46

Sierra Nuggets • Country-Style Chocolate Chip Cookies
Guittard® *(Guittard Chocolate Co.)*

Polka Dot Peanut Butter Jumbos
"M&M's" *(M&M/MARS)*

Solo® Kolacky
(Sokol & Company)

Wheat Germ Sour Cream Cookies
Elam's® *(Elam Mills)*

Gold'n Honey Nut Crunch Bars
Fisher® *(Fisher Nut Company)*

Double Chocolate Brownies, Easy Brownie Frosting *(top)*,
Saucepan Brownies *(bottom)*
Hershey's® *(Hershey Foods Corp.)*

Chocolate Almond Bark *(left)*, Creamy Chocolate Fudge *(right)*
Nestlé *(The Nestlé Company)*

Cane-Fest Pralines
Imperial *(Imperial Sugar Co.)*

Easy Homemade Chocolate Ice Cream
Eagle® Brand *(Borden Inc.)*

Blow-Away Sponge Cake
(Low Calorie/Low Fat)

½ cup cornstarch
2 tablespoons all-purpose flour
1 teaspoon baking powder
3 eggs
⅓ cup sugar
4 packets SWEET 'N LOW®
2 cups Delicious Whipped Topping*
12 medium-size fresh strawberries

Preheat oven to 375°F. Spray two 8-inch round layer pans with non-stick coating agent. Sift together cornstarch, flour, and baking powder. In separate deep bowl, beat eggs with electric mixer until foamy. Beat in sugar and SWEET 'N LOW® gradually, and continue beating 5 minutes or until mixture is very thick and lemon colored. Gently fold in dry ingredients, a few tablespoons at a time, mixing carefully and thoroughly. Turn mixture into prepared pans. Place in oven and reduce heat to 350°F. Bake 15 minutes, or until cake begins to shrink from sides of pan and top springs back when lightly pressed with finger. Let stand 1 or 2 minutes. Loosen sides and turn onto cooling rack. When cool, fill and frost with Delicious Whipped Topping. Top with strawberries.

Per Serving (¹⁄₁₂ of cake): Calories: 85; Fat: 2g

Note: There's no need to spray with a non-stick coating agent if you own non-stick 8-inch layer pans.

*Delicious Whipped Topping
(Low Calorie/Low Fat/Low Sodium)

¾ cup plain low-fat yogurt
½ cup part-skim ricotta cheese
1 teaspoon vanilla
2 packets SWEET 'N LOW®

In small deep bowl, beat yogurt and ricotta cheese with electric mixer until smooth and creamy. Add vanilla and SWEET 'N LOW® and continue beating until mixture is thoroughly blended. Mixture will keep in refrigerator several days. Rewhip before serving. Serve as frosting on cakes and as topping on pies or fruit desserts.

Per Serving (2 tablespoons): Calories: 15; Fat: 1g; Sodium: 15mg

Solo® Poppy Form Cake

1 cup butter or margarine, softened
1½ cups sugar
1 (12½ oz.) can SOLO® Poppy Filling
4 eggs, separated
1 teaspoon vanilla extract
1 cup dairy sour cream
2½ cups all-purpose flour
1 teaspoon baking soda
1 teaspoon salt
Confectioners sugar

Preheat oven to 350°F. Grease and lightly flour a 9- or 10-inch tube pan. Cream butter or margarine and sugar together until light and fluffy. Add SOLO® Poppy Filling. Add egg yolks, one at a time, beating well after each addition. Add vanilla and sour cream. Sift together flour, baking soda, and salt; add to mixture gradually, beating well after each addition. Beat egg whites until stiff but not dry; fold in batter. Turn batter into prepared pan. Bake about 1 hour and 10 to 15 minutes, or until a cake tester inserted in center of cake comes out clean. Allow cake to cool about 5 minutes. Remove from pan. To decorate, sift confectioners sugar through a paper doily or a cutout on the top of the cake.

Della Robbia Cake

1 package DUNCAN HINES® Deluxe Angel Food
   Cake Mix
1½ teaspoons grated lemon peel
6 tablespoons sugar
1½ tablespoons cornstarch
1 cup water
½ teaspoon vanilla extract
1 tablespoon lemon juice
Few drops red food coloring
6 canned cling peach slices
6 medium strawberries

Mix cake as directed on package except add grated lemon peel along with the cake flour mixture (red "B" packet). Bake and cool as directed.

Combine sugar, cornstarch, and water in a small saucepan. Cook over medium high heat until mixture thickens and clears. Remove from heat; add vanilla extract, lemon juice, and red food coloring. Alternate peach slices with strawberries around top of cake. Pour prepared glaze over fruit and top of cake. Refrigerate uncovered at least 1 hour. Store cake in refrigerator.

12 to 16 servings

Liquore Galliano
Harvey Wallbanger Cake

1 box orange cake mix (about 18½ oz.)
1 box (3¾ oz.) instant vanilla pudding mix
4 eggs
½ cup vegetable oil
5 oz. LIQUORE GALLIANO®
2 oz. vodka
5 oz. orange juice
1 cup confectioners sugar

Combine cake mix and pudding in a large bowl. Blend in eggs, oil, 4 oz. LIQUORE GALLIANO®, 1 oz. vodka, and 4 oz. orange juice. Mix batter until smooth and thick. Pour into a greased and floured 10″ Bundt® pan.* Bake at 350° for 45 minutes. Let cool in pan 10 minutes, then remove and place on rack. Have glaze ready to spoon on while cake is still warm.

GLAZE:
Combine confectioners sugar, remaining LIQUORE GAL-LIANO®, vodka and orange juice. Blend until very smooth.

*Or use two greased and floured 9″ cake pans. Bake at 350° for 30 minutes.

Peanut Butter Spice Cake

½ cup butter or margarine, softened
1 cup smooth or crunchy peanut butter
2 cups firmly-packed COLONIAL® Light Golden
    Brown Sugar
2 eggs
2½ cups unsifted flour
2 teaspoons baking soda
1 teaspoon salt
1 teaspoon ground cinnamon
¼ teaspoon ground cloves
2 cups applesauce
Peanut Butter Frosting*

Preheat oven to 350°. In large mixer bowl, cream together butter, peanut butter and sugar; beat in eggs. Combine dry ingredients. Add alternately with applesauce to sugar mixture, beating well after each addition. Pour into 2 greased 9-inch round cake pans. Bake 35 to 40 minutes or until cake springs back when lightly touched. Cool. Fill and frost with Peanut Butter Frosting.*

Makes one 9-inch 2-layer cake

*Peanut Butter Frosting

½ cup smooth or crunchy peanut butter
1 cup firmly-packed COLONIAL® Light Golden Brown
    Sugar
⅓ cup milk
3 cups COLONIAL® Confectioners' Sugar

In medium saucepan, melt peanut butter over very low heat. Blend in brown sugar and milk. Remove from heat; stir in confectioners' sugar.

Makes about 2½ cups

KAHLÚA®

Creamy Cake Kahlúa®

¼ pound butter, unsalted
3 oz. or ½ cup of almonds, finely chopped
⅓ cup sugar
1 egg yolk
½ tsp. vanilla
7 Tbsp. KAHLÚA® liqueur
1 pint whipping cream
18 lady fingers (36 halves)
2 tsp. powdered sugar

Combine butter, almonds, sugar, egg yolk, vanilla and 2 table-spoons KAHLÚA® in the bowl of an electric mixer and beat mixture for 15 minutes.

In a shallow dish, combine ⅓ cup cream and 1 tablespoon KAHLÚA®. Rapidly dip each ½ lady finger in the cream and KAHLÚA® mixture, making sure not to soak the lady fingers. Place 12 lady fingers on a serving tray side-by-side to form the first layer. Spread half of the butter and almond mixture over the lady finger layer. Place a second layer of 12 dipped lady fingers on the butter mixture and spread remaining butter mixture on the second layer of lady fingers. Top with the third layer of 12 dipped lady fingers. This now resembles a loaf-shaped cake.

(Continued)

Combine remaining cream, KAHLÚA® and powdered sugar and whip until stiff. Frost cake with whipped cream, top and sides. Place toothpicks in cake on top and gently cover with plastic wrap. Refrigerate overnight.

Chocolate Fans
(The crowning touch)

4 oz. semi-sweet chocolate
2 Tbsp. KAHLÚA®

Combine chocolate and KAHLÚA® in the top of a double boiler, over simmering water. Stir continually until chocolate has melted. Cover a cookie sheet with wax paper and draw two eight-inch circles on the paper. Spread the chocolate evenly inside the circles approximately ¼ inch thick. Chill in refrigerator until hard. Remove from refrigerator and allow to rest for a few minutes. Measure eight equal wedges and cut the chocolate. Arrange the wedges or fans on the top of the cake.   *Serves 6-8*

Colombian Fresh Banana Cake With Sea Foam Frosting

1 pkg. (18½ oz.) yellow cake mix*
⅛ teaspoon baking soda
2 eggs
¾ cup COCA-COLA®
1 cup (2 to 3) mashed ripe bananas
2 teaspoons lemon juice
⅓ cup finely chopped nuts, optional

In large mixing bowl combine mix, baking soda and eggs. Measure COCA-COLA®, stir briskly until foaming stops, and add to batter. Blend ingredients just until moistened, then beat at high speed of electric mixer for 3 minutes, scraping bowl often. Combine mashed bananas with lemon juice. Add to cake batter with nuts. Beat 1 minute at medium speed and turn into a generously greased and lightly floured 13×9×2-inch pan. Bake at 350°F about 40 minutes or until cake tests done. Cool on rack 15 minutes, remove cake from pan and turn right side up on rack to finish cooling.

*Do not use mix with pudding added or which requires oil.

Sea Foam Frosting

2 egg whites (¼ cup)
1½ cups firmly packed light brown sugar
⅛ teaspoon cream of tartar or 1 tablespoon light corn
    syrup
⅓ cup COCA-COLA®
1 teaspoon vanilla extract
Dash salt

In top of double boiler, combine all ingredients except vanilla and beat 1 minute at high speed of electric mixer. Place over boiling water (water should not touch bottom of top part); beat on high speed about 7 minutes until frosting forms peaks when beater is raised. Remove from boiling water (for smoothest frosting, empty into large bowl). Add vanilla and continue beating on high speed until thick enough to spread, about 2 minutes. Spread on sides and top of cold banana cake.

Brandy Pudding Cake

2 tablespoons butter for pan
⅓ cup finely chopped almonds
1 tablespoon sugar
1 (18½ ounce) package yellow cake mix
1 (3¾ ounce) package vanilla instant pudding mix
4 large eggs
⅓ cup California Brandy
⅔ cup water
½ cup butter, softened
1 tablespoon grated orange peel
Brandy Orange Glaze*

Butter 10-inch fluted tube cake pan well, using 2 tablespoons butter. Sprinkle with almonds and sugar. Combine cake mix, pudding mix, eggs, brandy, water and softened butter. Blend on low speed of electric mixer until moistened. Beat at medium speed for 2 minutes, scraping bowl frequently, until batter is smooth and well blended. Stir in orange peel. Turn into prepared pan. Bake below oven center in moderate oven (350 degrees F) 40 to 45 minutes, until pick inserted in center comes out clean. Remove from oven and let stand in pan 15 minutes, then invert onto wire rack to cool. When cold, drizzle with Brandy Orange Glaze.

Makes 1 large cake

*Brandy Orange Glaze

Melt 2 tablespoons butter. Stir in 1 tablespoon *each* California Brandy and orange juice, 1½ teaspoons grated orange peel and 1 cup sifted powdered sugar. *Makes ½ cup*

Favorite recipe from the **California Brandy Advisory Board**

Marble Chiffon Cake

⅓ cup HERSHEY'S® Unsweetened Cocoa
2 tablespoons sugar
¼ cup water
2 tablespoons vegetable oil
2 cups unsifted all-purpose flour
1½ cups sugar
3 teaspoons baking powder
1 teaspoon salt
½ cup vegetable oil
7 egg yolks
¾ cup cold water
2 teaspoons vanilla
7 egg whites
½ teaspoon cream of tartar

Combine cocoa, 2 tablespoons sugar, ¼ cup water, and 2 tablespoons oil in a small bowl; stir until smooth. Set aside. Combine flour, 1½ cups sugar, baking powder and salt in large mixer bowl. Add, in order, ½ cup vegetable oil, egg yolks, ¾ cup water and vanilla. Beat at low speed until combined, then at high speed 5 minutes.

With second set of beaters, beat egg whites in large mixer bowl with cream of tartar until stiff peaks form. Pour batter in a thin stream over entire surface of egg whites; fold in lightly by hand. Remove ⅓ batter to a separate bowl; gently fold in chocolate

mixture. Pour half the light batter into an ungreased 10-inch tube pan, top with half the dark batter. Repeat layers; with narrow spatula, swirl gently through batters to marble. Bake at 325° for 65-70 minutes or until done. Invert cake in pan; cool thoroughly. Loosen cake from pan; invert onto serving plate. Glaze with Vanilla Glaze*, if desired. *12 servings*

*Vanilla Glaze

Heat ¼ cup butter or margarine in saucepan until melted. Stir in 2 cups confectioners' sugar, 1 teaspoon vanilla and 2 to 3 tablespoons hot water or until desired consistency. Pour on top of cake allowing some to run down sides.

JELL-O®

Pistachio Pudding Cake

1 package (2-layer size) yellow cake mix*
1 package (4-serving size) JELL-O® Brand Pistachio Flavor Instant Pudding & Pie Filling
4 eggs
1¼ cups water*
¼ cup oil
½ teaspoon almond extract
7 drops green food coloring (optional)

Combine all ingredients in large mixer bowl. Blend; then beat at medium speed of electric mixer for 4 minutes. Pour into greased and floured 10-inch fluted tube or tube pan. Bake at 350° for 50 to 55 minutes or until cake tester inserted in center comes out clean and cake begins to pull away from sides of pan. *Do not underbake.* Cool in pan 15 minutes. Remove from pan and finish cooling on rack.

*Or use pudding-included cake mix and 1 cup water.

Heavenly Coconut Cake

Preheat oven to 325°. Grease and flour a tube pan. Sprinkle ½ cup chopped walnuts or pecans, mixed with ⅓ cup flaked coconut, on bottom and sides of pan. Combine the following ingredients:

1 (18.5 oz.) box yellow cake mix
1 small (3⅝ oz.) box instant vanilla pudding
4 eggs
½ cup cooking oil
½ cup water
½ cup COCO CASA™ Cream of Coconut

Beat 2 minutes with electric mixer. Bake about 1 hour. Remove from oven and punch holes on top of hot cake in pan. Pour half Coconut Sauce* mixture over cake. When cake cools, remove from pan, turn over and cover with other half Coconut Sauce mixture. Sprinkle with flaked coconut.

*Coconut Sauce

4 oz. butter
⅓ cup sugar
2 Tbsp. water
3 Tbsp. COCO CASA™ Cream of Coconut

Boil butter, sugar and water for 1 minute. Remove from flame and mix in **Cream of Coconut**.

COURVOISIER
The Brandy of Napoleon

Royal Courvoisier®
Pound Cake

2¼ cups flour
1 teaspoon baking powder
¼ teaspoon salt
2 sticks (1 cup) butter
1 cup sugar
6 egg yolks, lightly beaten
1 teaspoon vanilla extract
⅓ cup water
6 egg whites

Butter and line bottom of a 9-inch loaf pan with waxed paper. Sift flour, baking powder and salt twice. Cream the butter and add sugar gradually; beat until light and fluffy. Add the egg yolks and continue beating until mixture is very light. Gradually sift in flour, a little at a time, beating well. Stir in vanilla and water. Beat egg whites until stiff. Fold into flour mixture. Pour the batter in the prepared pan. Bake in a preheated 300°F. oven for 1¼ hours. Meanwhile, make the Orange **COURVOISIER**® Sauce*.

*Orange
Courvoisier® Sauce

⅓ cup sugar
1½ tablespoons cornstarch
1 cup orange juice
3 tablespoons butter
1 tablespoon grated orange rind
½ cup **COURVOISIER**® Brandy
¼ cup sliced almonds

Mix sugar and cornstarch in a small saucepan; add juice. Cook for five minutes over medium heat, stirring constantly. Add butter and stir until melted. Add orange rind and **COURVOISIER**®. Pour half the sauce over cake while sauce is still warm. Sprinkle with almonds. Pass the remaining sauce as the cake is served.

Makes 6 to 8 servings

KITCHENS OF
Sara Lee

Peaches 'n' Cream
Pound Cake

½ cup dairy sour cream
1 tablespoon orange liqueur OR orange juice
1 cup sliced sweetened fresh peaches, strawberries, OR nectarines
½ cup fresh blueberries
6 slices, each ½-inch thick, **SARA LEE Pound Cake**, thawed

Stir together sour cream and liqueur. Fold in fruit. Spoon about ¼ cup fruit mixture over each Pound Cake slice.

Makes 6 servings

Broiled-Fluff®-Frosting

⅓ cup butter or margarine, melted
1 cup **MARSHMALLOW FLUFF**®
⅛ tsp. salt
1 cup shredded coconut
½ cup chopped walnuts

Combine all ingredients; spread over the top of *hot* cake. Broil slowly, about 2 minutes until golden brown. Makes enough to frost one 9-inch square cake.

General Mills

Strawberry Shortcakes

2 pints strawberries, sliced
⅔ cup sugar
Shortcakes*
¾ cup chilled whipping cream

Sprinkle strawberries with sugar; let stand 1 hour. Bake Shortcakes. Beat whipping cream in chilled bowl until stiff. Split shortcakes; spoon strawberries between halves and over tops. Top with whipped cream.   *6 servings*

*Shortcakes

2⅓ cups **BISQUICK**® Baking Mix
½ cup milk
3 tablespoons sugar
3 tablespoons margarine or butter, melted

Heat oven to 425°. Mix all ingredients until soft dough forms. Gently smooth dough into ball on lightly floured cloth-covered board. Knead 8 to 10 times. Roll dough ½ inch thick. Cut with floured 3-inch cutter. Place on ungreased cookie sheet. Bake until golden brown, 10 to 12 minutes.

Towering Strawberry
Shortcake

10-oz. can **HUNGRY JACK**® **Refrigerated Flaky Biscuits**
2 tablespoons margarine or butter, melted
2 to 4 tablespoons sugar
1 pint (2 cups) fresh strawberries, sliced and sweetened
1 cup whipping cream, whipped or 2 cups whipped topping
Whole strawberries

Heat oven to 400°F. Grease a cookie sheet. Separate dough into 10 biscuits. Gently press 2 biscuits together for each shortcake. Dip top and sides of each in margarine; then in sugar. Place on prepared cookie sheet. Bake at 400°F. for 12 to 16 minutes or until golden brown. Cool slightly; split and fill with strawberries and whipped cream. Top with additional whipped cream and garnish with whole strawberry.   *5 servings*

KITCHENS OF Sara Lee

Strawberry Spiced Shortcake

6 frozen **SARA LEE Individual Cinnamon Raisin Danish**
½ cup whipping cream
1 tablespoon confectioners' sugar
2 packages (10-oz. each) frozen strawberries, thawed and drained

Warm Danish according to package directions. While Danish are warming, whip cream, gradually adding confectioners' sugar. Beat until stiff peaks form. TO SERVE TWO LAYER SHORT-CAKES: place 3 warm Danish on 3 plates, spoon about 1 table-spoon strawberries on each Danish. Top each serving with about 2 tablespoons of whipped cream. Repeat layers once. Makes 3 servings. OR TO SERVE SINGLE LAYER SHORTCAKES: place warm Danish on 6 plates, spoon about 1 tablespoon straw-berries on each Danish. Top with whipped cream.

Makes 6 servings

Jif

Jif® Peanut Butter Cupcakes

1 cup packed brown sugar
½ cup **JIF® Peanut Butter**
¼ cup butter or margarine, softened
2 eggs
1 teaspoon vanilla
1½ cups sifted all-purpose flour
2 teaspoons baking powder
½ teaspoon salt
½ cup milk
1 6-ounce package (1 cup) semisweet chocolate pieces or ¾ cup jelly

Preheat oven to 350°. Cream brown sugar, **JIF®**, and butter. Beat in eggs and vanilla. Mix flour, baking powder, and ½ teaspoon salt. Add to creamed mixture alternately with milk, mixing till blended.

Spoon a rounded tablespoonful of batter into greased muffin pans or paper bake cups in muffin pans. Place 10 to 12 chocolate pieces or 2 teaspoons jelly in center of each spoonful of batter. Top with a second tablespoonful of batter. Bake in 350° oven about 25 minutes or till done.

Makes 18

Guittard® Black Bottom Cupcakes

#1 MIXTURE:

Combine
    6 ounces cream cheese
    2 beaten eggs
    ¼ tsp. salt, ⅔ cup sugar
Beat well, stir in
    12 ounce pkg. **GUITTARD® Semi-Sweet Chocolate Chips**
Set above aside.

(Continued)

#2 MIXTURE:

Sift together
    3 cups flour
    ½ cup unsweetened cocoa
    2 tsp. baking soda
    2 cups sugar
    1 tsp. salt
Add
    2 cups water
    ⅔ cup cooking oil
    2 Tbsp. vinegar
    2 tsp. vanilla
Beat well together.

Fill 36 large cupcake liners with #2 mixture a little more than half. Drop one teaspoon #1 mixture on top of each. Bake at 350 degrees for 25 minutes.

Rolls & Coffee Cakes

Pineapple Pecan Rolls

3½ to 4 cups all-purpose flour
1 package **RED STAR® Instant Blend Dry Yeast**
2 tablespoons sugar
1 teaspoon salt
¾ cup milk
¼ cup water
¼ cup shortening
1 egg
½ cup plus 3 tablespoons pineapple preserves
2 tablespoons butter, softened
¼ cup brown sugar
⅓ cup pecans, chopped

Topping:

½ cup brown sugar
⅓ cup butter or margarine
2 tablespoons corn syrup
½ cup pecans, chopped

In large mixer bowl, combine 1½ cups flour, yeast, sugar and salt; mix well. In saucepan, heat milk, water and shortening until warm (120-130°; shortening does not need to melt). Add to flour mix-ture. Add egg. Blend at low speed until moistened; beat 3 minutes at medium speed. By hand, gradually stir in ½ cup pineapple preserves and enough remaining flour to make a soft dough. Knead on floured surface until smooth and elastic, about 5 min-utes. Place in greased bowl, turning to grease top. Cover; let rise in warm place until light and doubled, about 45 minutes.

In small saucepan, combine Topping ingredients. Heat until butter melts. Stir and pour into ungreased 13 × 9-inch pan; spread evenly.

Punch down dough. On lightly-floured surface, roll or pat to 18 × 9-inch rectangle. Spread with softened butter and 3 table-spoons preserves. Sprinkle with brown sugar and pecans. Starting with longer side, roll up tightly, pressing dough into roll with each turn. Pinch edges to seal. Cut into eighteen 1-inch slices. Place in prepared pan. Cover; let rise in warm place until doubled, about 45 minutes. Bake at 350° for 25 to 30 minutes. Cover pan with foil and invert onto rack. Cool 1 minute. Remove pan; cool.

18 Rolls

Cherry & Nut Swirls

2 packages (8 oz. each) cream cheese, softened
⅓ cup sugar
2 egg yolks
½ teaspoon vanilla extract
1 cup chopped **PLANTERS® Pecan Pieces**
1 cup chopped red candied cherries
5¾ to 6¼ cups unsifted flour
¾ cup sugar
1 teaspoon salt
3 packages **FLEISCHMANN'S® Active Dry Yeast**
1 cup water
½ cup (1 stick) margarine
3 eggs (at room temperature)
1 tablespoon margarine, melted

Beat together cream cheese and ⅓ cup sugar. Add egg yolks and vanilla; beat well. Add **PLANTERS® Pecan Pieces** and cherries; beat until cheese mixture becomes pink in color. Refrigerate until ready to use.

In a large bowl thoroughly mix 1¾ cups flour, ¾ cup sugar, salt and undissolved **FLEISCHMANN'S® Active Dry Yeast.**

Combine water and margarine in a saucepan. Heat over low heat until very warm (120°F.-130°F.). Margarine does not need to melt. Gradually add to dry ingredients and beat 2 minutes at medium speed of electric mixer, scraping bowl occasionally. Add eggs and ¾ cup flour. Beat at high speed 2 minutes, scraping bowl occasionally. Stir in enough additional flour to make a soft dough. Turn out onto lightly floured board; knead until smooth and elastic, about 8 to 10 minutes.

Divide dough into 3 equal pieces. Roll out one piece to a 12 × 10-inch rectangle. Spread ⅓ of prepared cheese filling over dough to within ½-inch of the long ends. Roll up like a jelly roll from long end. Cut into 12 1-inch thick slices. Place rolls on baking sheet and cover with plastic wrap. Place in freezer. Repeat with remaining dough and filling. When rolls are frozen, place in plastic bags in groups of twelve. Freeze up to 4 weeks.

For 1 dozen rolls remove 1 bag from freezer; unwrap. Loosely cover and let stand at room temperature until fully thawed, about 1 hour and 15 minutes. With palm of hand, flatten rolls out to 2½-inch circles. Place on greased baking sheet. Cover; let rise in warm place, free from draft, until doubled in bulk, about 1 hour and 30 minutes.

Brush with melted margarine. Bake at 350°F. for 12 to 15 minutes, or until done. Let cool 10 minutes before removing from baking sheet. Continue cooling on wire rack. Decorate as desired. *Makes 3 dozen*

To bake without freezing: After shaping rolls, cover and let rise in a warm place, free from draft, until doubled in bulk, about 1 hour and 15 minutes. Bake as directed above.

Solo® Kolacky

1 cup butter or margarine, softened
1 (8-ounce) package cream cheese, softened
1 tablespoon milk
1 tablespoon sugar
1 egg yolk, well beaten
1½ cups all-purpose flour
½ teaspoon baking powder
1 (#1 can) **SOLO® Cake and Pastry Filling**
Confectioners sugar

Cream butter or margarine, cream cheese, milk, and sugar together. Add egg yolk. Sift together flour and baking powder. Add to creamed mixture and blend well. Refrigerate for several hours or overnight. Preheat oven to 400°F. Turn dough out on a lightly floured board and roll to a ¼-inch thickness. Cut with a cookie cutter and make a depression with thumb or spoon in center of each. Place 1 teaspoon **SOLO® Cake and Pastry Filling** into each center. Bake 10 to 12 minutes, or until lightly browned. Sprinkle with confectioners sugar before serving.

About 3 dozen

Kolache
(koh-lotch-eh)

3 to 3½ cups all-purpose flour
1 package **RED STAR® Instant Blend Dry Yeast**
¼ cup sugar
1 teaspoon salt
¾ cup milk
¼ cup water
¼ cup butter or margarine
1 egg
1 tablespoon butter

In large mixer bowl, combine 1½ cups flour, yeast, sugar and salt; mix well. In saucepan, heat milk, water and butter until warm (120-130°; butter does not need to melt). Add to flour mixture. Add egg. Blend at low speed until moistened; beat 3 minutes at medium speed. By hand, gradually stir in enough remaining flour to make a soft dough. Knead on floured surface until smooth and elastic, about 3 minutes. Place in greased bowl, turning to grease top. Cover; let rise in warm place until light and doubled, about 1 hour.

Punch down dough. Divide into 2 parts. On lightly floured surface, roll each half to a 12-inch square. Cut each square into nine 4-inch squares. Spoon Filling (recipe follows) in center of each square. Fold one corner to the center. Moisten corner of dough with water. Fold opposite corner over and seal. Place on greased cookie sheets. Cover; let rise in warm place until almost double, about 15 minutes. Brush with butter. Bake at 375° for 12 to 15 minutes until golden brown. Remove from cookie sheets. Serve warm or cold. *18 Kolaches*

FILLING VARIATIONS:
Prune Orange Filling

1 cup prunes (¾ cup puréed)
⅓ cup orange marmalade
⅓ cup chopped nuts
1 teaspoon lemon juice

In small saucepan, cover prunes with water. Cook until tender. Remove seeds. Purée prunes in blender. In small bowl, blend prunes, marmalade and nuts. Add lemon juice. Use about 1 tablespoon filling for each Kolache.

Filling for 18 Kolaches Makes 1½ cups

Cream Cheese Raisin Filling

2 packages (3 oz. each) cream cheese, softened
2 tablespoons sugar
1 egg
1 teaspoon lemon rind
¼ cup golden raisins, chopped

In small mixer bowl, combine cream cheese, sugar, egg and lemon rind. Beat until smooth and creamy. Stir in raisins. Use about 2 teaspoons filling for each Kolache.

Filling for 18 Kolaches Makes 1 cup

Apricot Almond Filling

1 cup dried apricot halves
⅓ cup packed brown sugar
⅓ cup chopped almonds
½ teaspoon cinnamon

In small saucepan, cover apricot halves with water. Cook over medium heat until water is absorbed and apricots are tender. Purée apricots in blender. In small bowl, combine apricots, brown sugar, almonds, and cinnamon. Use about 2½ teaspoons filling for each Kolache.

Filling for 18 Kolaches Makes 1¼ cups

Cranberry Orange Filling

⅔ cup canned (ready-to-serve) cranberry orange relish
⅓ cup vanilla wafer crumbs
¼ cup chopped nuts
Dash cinnamon

In small bowl, combine ingredients. Use about 2 teaspoons filling for each Kolache.

Filling for 18 Kolaches Makes 1 cup

Overnight Cinnamon Rolls

2 packages active dry yeast
½ cup warm water (105 to 115°)
2 cups lukewarm milk (scalded then cooled)
⅓ cup sugar
⅓ cup vegetable oil or shortening
3 teaspoons baking powder
2 teaspoons salt
1 egg
6½ to 7½ cups GOLD MEDAL® All-Purpose Flour*
4 tablespoons margarine or butter, softened
½ cup sugar
1 tablespoon plus 1 teaspoon ground cinnamon
Powdered Sugar Frosting (recipe follows)

Dissolve yeast in warm water in large bowl. Stir in milk, ⅓ cup sugar, the oil, baking powder, salt, egg and 2 to 3 cups of the flour. Beat until smooth. Mix in enough remaining flour to make dough easy to handle. Turn dough onto well-floured surface; knead until smooth and elastic, 8 to 10 minutes. Place in greased bowl; turn greased side up. Cover; let rise in warm place until double, about 1½ hours. (Dough is ready if indentation remains when touched.)

Grease 2 rectangular pans, 13x9x2 inches. Punch down dough; divide into halves. Roll 1 half into rectangle, 12x10 inches. Spread with 2 tablespoons of the margarine. Mix ½ cup sugar and the cinnamon; sprinkle half the sugar-cinnamon mixture over rectangle. Roll up, beginning at 12-inch side. Pinch edge of dough into roll to seal. Stretch roll to make even.

Cut roll into twelve 1-inch slices. Place slightly apart in 1 pan. Wrap pan tightly with heavy-duty aluminum foil. Repeat with remaining dough. Refrigerate at least 12 hours but no longer than 48 hours. (To bake immediately, do not wrap. Let rise in warm place until double, about 30 minutes.) Heat oven to 350°. Remove foil from pans. Bake until golden, 30 to 35 minutes. Frost with Powdered Sugar Frosting while warm.

2 dozen rolls

*If using self-rising flour, omit baking powder and salt.

(Continued)

Powdered Sugar Frosting

Mix 1 cup powdered sugar, 1 tablespoon milk and ½ teaspoon vanilla until smooth and of spreading consistency. Frosts 1 pan of rolls.

Note: Unbleached flour can be used in this recipe.

Note: If larger rolls are desired, roll dough into rectangles, 10x9 inches. Cut each roll into 9 slices. Place in greased square pans 9x9x2 inches.

18 rolls

Sourdough Cinnamon Rolls

1 cup warm low-fat milk
1 package active dry yeast (check the date on the package)
1 teaspoon vanilla extract
½ cup SWEETLITE™ Fructose
¼ cup melted corn oil margarine
2 eggs lightly beaten
1 package BATTER-LITE® Natural Sourdough Bread Mix
1 teaspoon salt
3½ cups unbleached white flour
Melted corn oil margarine
1 tablespoon cinnamon
½ cup SWEETLITE™ Fructose
1 package FROSTLITE™ White Frosting Mix

1. Pour the warm milk into a large warm mixing bowl and sprinkle the yeast over the top of it. Stir until the yeast is dissolved, about 5 minutes

2. Add ½ cup fructose, lightly beaten eggs and ¼ cup melted margarine and mix well.

3. Add the **BATTER-LITE® Natural Sourdough Bread Mix** and mix well.

4. Combine the salt and flour. Add 3 cups of the flour mixture, ½ cup at a time, mixing thoroughly. Turn onto a floured board and knead the dough, adding the remaining flour mixture until the dough is no longer sticky and is easy to handle, and still a soft dough.

5. Roll out approximately 14″ x 14″ and ½″ thick. Brush with melted margarine.

6. Combine the cinnamon and ¼ cup fructose and sprinkle generously over the dough.

7. Form into an even long roll. Cut into slices approximately 1″ wide and place each slice onto a lightly oiled cookie sheet. Place on the pan so that the sides touch.

8. Let rise in a warm place until doubled in volume, about 45 minutes. The oven of a gas stove or an electric oven with the light on provides the right warmth.

9. Preheat the oven to 375°. Bake for 20-25 minutes. Remove from the oven.

10. Prepare the **FROSTLITE™ White Frosting Mix** according to package directions. Spread evenly over the tops of the rolls while they are still warm.

Makes 20 cinnamon rolls

VARIATION:

Pecan Rolls

Add ½ cup finely chopped pecans after step 6, sprinkling them evenly over the cinnamon-fructose mixture just before forming the roll.

Cranberry-Almond Braid

5¾ to 6¼ cups unsifted flour
¾ cup sugar
1 teaspoon salt
3 packages FLEISCHMANN'S® Active Dry Yeast
½ cup (1 stick) margarine, softened
1 cup very warm water (120°F.-130°F.)
3 eggs (at room temperature)
Confectioners' sugar frosting
PLANTERS® Sliced Almonds

Prepare Cranberry Filling.* Refrigerate until ready to use. In a large bowl thoroughly mix 1¼ cups flour, sugar, salt and undissolved FLEISCHMANN'S® Active Dry Yeast. Add softened margarine.

Gradually add very warm water to dry ingredients and beat 2 minutes at medium speed of electric mixer, scraping bowl occasionally. Add eggs and ¼ cup flour. Beat at high speed 2 minutes, scraping bowl occasionally. Stir in enough additional flour to make a soft dough. Turn out onto lightly floured board; knead until smooth and elastic, about 8 to 10 minutes.

Divide dough into 3 equal pieces. Roll one piece into a 12-inch square. Cut into 3 lengthwise strips, 12 × 4-inches each. Spread centers of strips with ⅓ prepared Cranberry Filling. Seal edges and ends very firmly forming long filled ropes. Braid ropes together. Pinch ends to seal; tuck underneath. Place on greased baking sheet. Cover tightly with plastic wrap; place in freezer. Repeat with remaining pieces of dough and filling. When firm, remove from baking sheets and wrap each braid with plastic wrap, then with aluminum foil. Keep frozen up to 4 weeks.

Remove from freezer; unwrap and place on ungreased baking sheets. Let stand covered loosely with plastic wrap at room temperature until fully thawed, about 2 hours. Let rise in warm place, free from draft, until more than doubled in bulk, about 1¾ hours.

Bake at 375°F. for 15 to 20 minutes, or until done. Remove from baking sheets and cool on wire racks. Frost with confectioners' sugar frosting and decorate with PLANTERS® Sliced Almonds.   *Makes 3 loaves*

To bake without freezing: After shaping, let rise in a warm place, free from draft, until doubled in bulk, about 1 hour. Bake as directed above.

*Cranberry Filling

Combine 1½ cups ground fresh cranberries, a large ground fresh orange and 1 cup firmly packed dark brown sugar in a saucepan. Bring to a boil; reduce heat and simmer until thickened, stirring occasionally.

Simple Stollen

8-oz. pkg. cream cheese, softened
¼ cup sugar
1½ to 2 teaspoons rum flavoring
¼ cup chopped blanched almonds
½ cup raisins
¼ cup chopped maraschino cherries
2 (8-oz.) cans PILLSBURY Refrigerated Quick
   Crescent Dinner Rolls

Glaze:

1 cup powdered sugar
2 tablespoons milk
Candied red and green cherries, if desired

Heat oven to 375°F. In small bowl, beat cream cheese and sugar until fluffy. Stir in rum flavoring. Fold in almonds, raisins and cherries. Set aside.

Unroll the 2 cans of dough into 4 long rectangles on ungreased cookie sheet. Overlap long sides; firmly press perforations and edges to seal. Pat to form a 13 × 13-inch square. Spread cream cheese filling crosswise, in a 6-inch wide strip, down center of dough to within 1-inch of ends. Fold ends of dough 1-inch over filling. Bring sides of dough square over filling overlapping edges, forming a 6 × 11-inch loaf. Bake at 375°F. for 25 to 30 minutes or until light golden brown. Cool. Combine powdered sugar and milk; drizzle over top of cooled bread. Garnish with candied red and green cherries, if desired. Refrigerate leftovers.

12 to 14 slices

Wheat Germ Almond Cake

1 cup unsifted ROBIN HOOD® All Purpose Flour
¾ cup KRETSCHMER Wheat Germ, Regular or
   Brown Sugar & Honey
⅓ cup sugar
¼ tsp. salt
½ cup butter or margarine
2 Tbsp. milk
⅔ cup raspberry *or* apricot preserves

Batter:

1 cup ground natural almonds (¾ cup whole almonds)
½ cup KRETSCHMER Wheat Germ, Regular or
   Brown Sugar & Honey
½ cup unsifted ROBIN HOOD® All Purpose Flour
¼ tsp. salt
6 eggs, separated
¾ cup sugar
1 tsp. vanilla
½ tsp. almond extract

Combine 1 cup flour, ¾ cup wheat germ, ⅓ cup sugar and ¼ teaspoon salt in bowl. Stir well to blend. Cut in butter until mixture looks like coarse meal. Stir in milk. Press mixture evenly onto bottom and 2 inches up sides of 9-inch springform pan. Bake at 400° for 10 minutes. Remove from oven. Reduce temperature to 350°. Spread preserves over baked pastry.

BATTER:
Combine ground almonds, ½ cup wheat germ, ½ cup flour and ¼ teaspoon salt on wax paper. Stir well to blend. Beat egg yolks with ¾ cup sugar until thick and smooth. Beat in flavorings. Add blended dry ingredients, mixing until well-blended.

Beat egg whites until stiff peaks form. Fold half the whites into egg mixture. Fold in remaining whites. Pour into pastry shell. Bake at 350° for 60-65 minutes until cake tester inserted in center comes out clean. Cool for 1 hour. Remove sides of pan. Spread with Almond Glaze*.   *Makes 12-16 servings*

*Almond Glaze

¼ cup butter or margarine
¼ cup sugar
2 Tbsp. light corn syrup
2 tsp. unsifted ROBIN HOOD® All Purpose Flour
½ cup sliced natural almonds

Melt butter in small saucepan. Stir in sugar, corn syrup and flour. Heat to boiling, stirring constantly. Remove from heat. Stir in almonds.

Can Can Date-Nut Bread

1 8 oz. package **BORDO Imported Diced Dates**
¾ cup raisins
1 teaspoon baking soda
1 cup boiling water
2 tablespoons soft butter
1 cup sugar
1 teaspoon vanilla
1 egg
1⅓ cups flour
¾ cup chopped pecans

Place dates and raisins in covered bowl. Add soda and boiling water. Cover and let stand. Cream butter and sugar. Add vanilla. Add egg and beat well. Add flour, mix until moistened. Pour in fruit mixture, including liquid and pecans, and mix gently to prevent crushing the fruits.

Place a small amount of butter in the bottom of each of five empty condensed soup cans. Let the butter melt in the cans in the oven for a few minutes, before filling with batter. Then fill cans ⅔ full. Bake at 325° for 45 minutes or until cake tests done. Remove from can while warm.

If you prefer to make this recipe in a 9 × 5 inch loaf pan, butter the bottom of pan. Add batter. Bake at 350° for 45-55 minutes, or until cake tests done.

Chocolate Chip Coffee Cake

½ cup milk
½ cup (1 stick) **FLEISCHMANN'S® Margarine**
⅓ cup sugar
1 teaspoon salt
2 packages **FLEISCHMANN'S® Active Dry Yeast**
½ cup warm water (105°F.-115°F.)
2 eggs, beaten (at room temperature)
3 cups unsifted flour
½ cup semi-sweet real chocolate morsels

Scald milk; stir in **FLEISCHMANN'S® Margarine**, sugar and salt. Cool to lukewarm. Sprinkle **FLEISCHMANN'S® Active Dry Yeast** into warm water in a large bowl. Stir until dissolved. Add lukewarm milk mixture, eggs and 2 cups flour. Beat at medium speed of electric mixer until smooth, about 15 seconds. Stir in remaining 1 cup flour and chocolate morsels until well blended, about 1 minute. Turn into a well greased 10-inch tube pan. Cover and let rise in warm place, free from draft, until doubled in bulk, about 1½ hours. Bake at 400°F. for 20 minutes; remove from oven and sprinkle with Coffeecake Topping.* Return to oven and bake additional 15 minutes, or until done. Turn out of pan immediately and let cool on wire rack.

Makes 1 10-inch tube cake

FOOD PROCESSOR METHOD:
With metal blade in place combine flour, **FLEISCHMANN'S® Margarine**, sugar and salt in bowl; process 5 to 10 seconds to combine. Dissolve **FLEISCHMANN'S® Active Dry Yeast** in warm water; pour through feed tube. Add eggs. Begin processing, pouring cold milk through feed tube in a fast stream until ball forms, about 10-15 seconds. Continue processing for 30 seconds to knead batter. Mix in chocolate morsels.

Carefully remove dough from processor bowl. Turn out into a well greased 10-inch tube pan. Let rise and bake as directed above.

(Continued)

*Coffee Cake Topping

⅓ cup unsifted flour
½ cup chopped **PLANTERS® Pecans**
½ cup semi-sweet real chocolate morsels
⅓ cup sugar
¼ cup (½ stick) **FLEISCHMANN'S® Margarine**
1½ teaspoons cinnamon

Combine topping ingredients and rub together with fingers, until crumbly. Sprinkle on top of dough last 15 minutes of cooking.

FOOD PROCESSOR METHOD:
With metal blade in place process **PLANTERS® Pecans** for 3 to 5 seconds, until chopped. Add flour, chocolate morsels, sugar, **FLEISCHMANN'S® Margarine** and cinnamon; process 5 seconds until crumbly.

German Sweet Bread

½ cup butter or margarine, softened
1⅓ cups sugar
3 eggs
1 teaspoon vanilla
1 cup **BLUE RIBBON® Slivered Almonds**
2 squares (1 oz. each) unsweetened chocolate, finely chopped
1 cup vacuum-packed regular wheat germ
½ cup dark seedless raisins
½ cup diced mixed glacé fruit
1½ cups flour
1 teaspoon baking powder
½ teaspoon salt
1 cup milk

Cream butter with sugar; beat in eggs and vanilla. Mix almonds with chocolate, wheat germ, raisins, fruit, flour, baking powder and salt; stir into creamed mixture alternately with milk. Turn into well-greased and floured 7 to 9-cup crown or turban mold with hole in center. Bake 1 hour at 350 degrees or until a cake tester or long pick comes out dry. Cool 20 minutes in mold; invert and cool on wire rack. Decorate with powdered sugar glaze, chocolate curls, whole blanched almonds and candied violets, if you like.

Makes 1 loaf

Pies

Fresh Strawberry Yogurt Pie

2 cups **DANNON® Strawberry Yogurt**
½ cup crushed strawberries
1 container (8 oz. or 9 oz.) thawed **BIRDS EYE® COOL WHIP® Non-Dairy Whipped Topping**
1 graham cracker pie crust

Thoroughly combine crushed fruit and yogurt in bowl. Fold in **COOL WHIP®**, blending well. Spoon into crust and freeze about 4 hours. Remove from freezer and place in refrigerator 30 minutes (or longer for softer texture) before serving. Store any leftover pie in freezer.

Fresh Strawberry Pie

8 oz. **CONTINENTAL Strawberry Glaze**
1½ pints fresh strawberries
1 9 inch pre-baked pie shell
Whipped topping

Wash berries, remove stems and drain well. Pour glaze over berries in mixing bowl and tumble gently until berries are coated. Pour glazed berries into pie shell and smooth out to the edges. Refrigerate one hour before serving and decorate with whipped topping before slicing.

Joy Choy Pie

3 egg whites
¼ teaspoon cream of tartar
1 cup sugar
1 teaspoon vanilla
1 cup **LA CHOY® Chow Mein Noodles**, crushed
1 cup chopped pecans
1 pint fresh strawberries, sliced, OR
1 package (10 oz.) frozen sliced strawberries, partially thawed
1 cup whipping cream, whipped, sweetened

Beat egg whites until frothy. Add cream of tartar and beat until stiff but not dry. Add sugar a tablespoon at a time; continue to beat until stiff peaks form. Fold in vanilla. Gradually fold in chow mein noodles and pecans. Spoon into well-buttered 9-inch pie pan. Spread over bottom and sides of pie pan to form a shell. Bake at 325 degrees for 25 to 30 minutes. Cook completely on wire cake rack. Fill center with strawberries. Top with whipped cream.

6 servings

Orange Drambuie® Pie

2 tablespoons cornstarch
1 cup orange juice
5 egg yolks
¼ cup sugar
1 envelope unflavored gelatin
1 tablespoon butter
⅓ cup **DRAMBUIE®**
¾ cup heavy cream
9-inch prebaked pie shell
2 very small navel oranges
½ cup orange marmalade or apricot jelly

Mix cornstarch with ½ cup orange juice in a medium size bowl. Add the egg yolks and sugar; beat well. Pour remaining ½ cup juice in a medium saucepan. Sprinkle on gelatin, and bring to a boil, stirring until gelatin is dissolved. Remove from heat. Gradually stir a few spoons of hot juice into the egg yolk mixture. Then combine both mixtures in the saucepan. Return to heat and cook 3 minutes more stirring constantly. Remove from the heat and stir in the butter until melted; add **DRAMBUIE®**.

Cool rapidly over ice, then place in refrigerator until completely cool. Whip cream until thick; fold the cream into the cooled mixture and pour into pie shell. Melt the marmalade over low heat. Slice the oranges, unpeeled, into very thin rounds. Dip each slice

in melted jelly. Starting at the outside arrange the slices on top of the pie, overlapping each slice, and covering the entire top. Refrigerate until ready to serve. *Makes 6 to 8 servings*

Fruit Glacé Pie

1 **KEEBLER® READY-CRUST® Graham Cracker Pie Crust**
1 package (3 ounces) cream cheese, softened
2 tablespoons honey
1 medium banana, sliced
2 cups prepared mixed fruit: sliced peaches, seedless grapes, blueberries, strawberries, sweet cherries (pitted and halved), melon (cut in ½-inch pieces), canned pineapple chunks (well-drained), canned mandarin orange sections (well-drained)
1 package (4-serving size) peach flavor gelatin
¾ cup boiling water
2 cups ice cubes

Beat cream cheese and honey until smooth and creamy. Spread on bottom and sides of crust, covering completely. Chill while preparing fruit. Wash and drain fresh fruit; pat dry. Cut or slice large pieces. Layer banana slices in bottom of crust. Arrange mixed fruit decoratively on top. Prepare gelatin using quick-set method as follows: Dissolve gelatin using only ¾ cup boiling water; add ice cubes and stir until gelatin is thickened, about 3-4 minutes. Remove unmelted ice. Spoon gelatin over fruit to glaze. Do not overfill. Chill pie until set, about 1 hour.

Note: To use frozen fruit, prepare as follows:

Layer banana slices in bottom of crust. Prepare gelatin using quick-set method by dissolving gelatin in ¾ cup boiling water; add a 10 oz. package of frozen mixed fruit and stir until thickened, about 3-4 minutes. Pour into crust. Chill pie until set, about 1 hour.

Peaches and Cream Pie

1 (9-inch) **BANQUET® Deep Dish Frozen Pie Crust Shell**
1 (9-inch) **BANQUET® Frozen Pie Crust Shell**
5 to 6 medium peaches, sliced (about 4 cups)*
1 cup sugar, divided
5 tablespoons flour
⅛ teaspoon salt
½ cup dairy sour cream
¼ teaspoon cinnamon

Thaw frozen deep dish pie crust at room temperature for 10 minutes. Pop other frozen pie crust out of foil pan. Place upside down on waxed paper to thaw, about 10 minutes. Spread sliced peaches in bottom of deep dish pie crust. Place all but 2 tablespoons sugar in small mixing bowl. Add flour, salt and sour cream; stir until smooth. Spread evenly over peaches.

Flatten thawed pie crust on waxed paper by gently pressing down. Place on top of pie. Crimp edges to seal. Combine cinnamon and remaining 2 tablespoons sugar. Sprinkle on top of pie. Cut several 1-inch slits in top crust. Place a 2-inch strip of foil around crimped edges to prevent over browning. Bake pie on cookie sheet in 400°F oven for 40 to 45 minutes, until golden brown. Cool 30 minutes before serving. *Makes 6 servings*

*Substitution: Use 2 cans (1 lb. ea.) sliced peaches, drained or 1 bag (20 oz.) sliced frozen peaches for fresh sliced peaches.

Crisco

Fluffy Berry Cheese Pie

CRISCO® Pastry for single-crust 9-inch pie*
1 cup miniature marshmallows
½ cup milk
1 package (3 ounces) strawberry-flavored gelatin
½ cup water
1 package (3 ounces) cream cheese, softened
1 package (10 ounces) frozen strawberries, thawed
½ cup whipping cream

Line 9-inch pie plate with pastry; bake and cool. In saucepan, heat miniature marshmallows and milk over medium-low heat, stirring frequently, till marshmallows are melted; set aside. In small saucepan, combine strawberry-flavored gelatin and water. Heat and stir till gelatin is dissolved. Combine marshmallow mixture and gelatin; gradually beat into the softened cream cheese. Drain thawed strawberries, reserving syrup. Add water to syrup to equal ¾ cup liquid. Stir strawberry syrup into gelatin mixture; chill till mixture is partially set. Whip gelatin mixture; fold in strawberries. Whip the cream; fold into the whipped gelatin mixture. Chill again till mixture mounds when spooned. Pile strawberry mixture into the baked pastry shell. Chill 3 to 4 hours or till filling is set. Garnish with dollops of additional whipped cream and strawberries, if desired.

*Crisco® Pastry for Single-Crust Pie

1⅓ cups sifted flour
½ teaspoon salt
½ cup **CRISCO® Shortening**
2 to 3 tablespoons water

In mixing bowl, combine flour and salt. Cut in **CRISCO®** with pastry blender or two knives until mixture is uniform (mixture should be fairly coarse). Sprinkle with water, a tablespoon at a time; toss lightly with fork. When all water has been added, work dough into a firm ball.

Press dough into a flat circle with smooth edges. On lightly floured board or pastry cloth, roll dough to a circle ⅛ inch thick and about 1½ inches larger than inverted pie plate. Gently ease dough into the pie plate, being careful not to stretch the dough. Trim ½ inch beyond edge of pie plate. Fold under to make double thickness around rim. Flute edge of pastry as desired.

To bake without filling: Preheat oven to 425°. Prick bottom and sides of crust with fork. Bake 10 to 15 minutes or till lightly browned.

To bake with filling: Preheat oven to temperature stated in recipe. Do not prick dough. Bake according to recipe directions.

Coconut Cream Pie

Mix 1 box (4¾ oz.) vanilla pudding. Cool slightly. Add 1 cup fresh shredded **CALAVO® Coconut**. Pour into baked 9-inch pie shell. Cool. Cover with meringue made of 3 stiffly beaten egg whites, 6 tablespoons sugar. Sprinkle ½ cup shredded coconut on meringue. Bake in moderate oven (300°) for 12-15 minutes.

Kellogg's

Fluffy Orange-Lemon Pie

Crust:
¾ cup **KELLOGG'S® ALL-BRAN®** or **KELLOGG'S® BRAN BUDS®** Cereal
¾ cup finely chopped nuts
¼ cup margarine or butter, melted
3 tablespoons sifted confectioner's sugar

1 can (5.3 oz., ⅔ cup) evaporated milk
Water
1 can (11 oz., 1⅓ cups) mandarin orange segments, drained, reserving syrup
1 package (3 oz.) lemon flavor gelatin dessert

1. Crush **KELLOGG'S® ALL-BRAN® Cereal** to crumbs. Stir in nuts, margarine and sugar. Press mixture evenly in 9-inch glass pie plate to form crust.
2. Bake at 375°F for 6 to 8 minutes or until lightly browned. Cool completely. Chill.
3. Pour evaporated milk into small bowl of electric mixer. Place in freezer until ice crystals form around edge.
4. Meanwhile, add water to reserved mandarin orange syrup to measure 1¼ cups liquid. Bring to boil in small saucepan. Add gelatin, stirring until dissolved. Pour into large bowl of electric mixer. Chill until slightly thickened.
5. Beat thickened gelatin until frothy. Add orange segments, reserving some for garnish. Beat well. Beat milk until soft peaks form. Fold into gelatin mixture. Pour into cereal crust. Chill until firm. Garnish with reserved orange segments.

® Kellogg Company

Yield: 8 servings

Cranberry-Apple Pie

Crust:
1½ cups flour
Dash of salt
½ cup shortening
1½ cups (6 oz.) shredded **CRACKER BARREL Brand Sharp Natural Cheddar Cheese**
4 to 6 tablespoons water

Filling:
1½ cups sugar
3 tablespoons quick-cooking tapioca
½ teaspoon cinnamon
2 cups cranberries
⅓ cup water
6 cups peeled apple slices
1 tablespoon **PARKAY Margarine**

Combine flour and salt; cut in shortening until mixture resembles coarse crumbs. Stir in cheese. Sprinkle with water while mixing lightly with a fork; form into a ball. Divide dough in half. Roll one part to 11-inch circle on lightly floured surface. Place in 9-inch pie plate.

Combine sugar, tapioca and cinnamon. Stir in cranberries and water. Cook, stirring constantly, until mixture boils. Remove from heat; stir in apples. Cool slightly. Spoon into pastry shell; dot with margarine. Roll out remaining dough to 11-inch circle; place over fruit mixture. Seal edges of crusts and flute. Cut slits in top of pastry. Bake at 400°, 45 to 50 minutes or until apples are tender.

Apple Snow Pie

Crust:
1 Stay Fresh Pack **NABISCO** or **HONEY MAID**
  Graham Crackers, finely rolled (about 1⅔ cups)
¼ cup granulated sugar
⅓ cup butter or margarine, softened

Filling:
1 envelope unflavored gelatin
¼ cup water
3 eggs, separated
⅓ cup granulated sugar
1½ cups unsweetened applesauce
1 tablespoon lemon juice
1½ teaspoons lemon rind

Garnish:
¾ cup seedless green grapes, halved
1 (4⅝-ounce) can **SNACK MATE** American
  Pasteurized Process Cheese Spread

1. MAKE CRUST:
Preheat oven to 375°F. In medium bowl, using fork or pastry blender, combine graham cracker crumbs and sugar; blend in butter or margarine. Using back of large spoon, press mixture firmly into 9-inch pie plate to form crust. Bake 8 minutes; let stand on wire rack to cool.

2. MAKE FILLING:
In small saucepan, sprinkle gelatin over water; let stand 5 minutes to soften. Heat gently over very low heat, stirring to dissolve. In small bowl, beat egg yolks with a little hot gelatin mixture; return mixture to saucepan. Heat gently 30 seconds, stirring constantly.

3. In large bowl, with electric mixer at high speed, beat egg whites until soft peaks form. Gradually add sugar, 2 tablespoons at a time, beating until egg whites are stiff.

4. In medium bowl, blend applesauce, lemon juice and lemon rind; stir in egg-yolk mixture. Using a rubber spatula, gently fold in egg-white mixture. Spoon evenly into pie shell; chill 3 to 4 hours or until firm.

5. TO GARNISH:
Decorate top of pie with alternating circles of grape halves and **SNACK MATE Cheese** rosettes.   *Makes 6 to 8 servings*

Apple Pie

1 recipe double crust pastry*
¾ cup sugar
1 tablespoon **ARGO®/KINGSFORD'S® Corn Starch**
1 teaspoon ground cinnamon
2 pounds apples, peeled, cored, sliced (about 6 cups)
1 tablespoon lemon juice
1 tablespoon **MAZOLA®/NUCOA® Margarine**

Line 9-inch pie plate with one-half pastry rolled to ⅛-inch thickness, allowing 1-inch overhang. In large bowl stir together sugar, corn starch and cinnamon. Toss with apple slices and lemon juice

until coated. Turn into pie plate. Dot with margarine. Roll remaining pastry to 12-inch circle. Make several slits to permit steam to escape. Cover pie with pastry; seal and flute edge. Bake in 425°F oven 50 minutes or until crust is golden and apples are tender.
Makes 1 (9-inch) pie

*Double Crust Pie

½ cup **MAZOLA® Corn Oil**
¼ cup skim milk
2 cups unsifted flour
1 teaspoon salt

In measuring cup stir together corn oil and milk. In large bowl stir together flour and salt. Add corn oil mixture stirring constantly with fork. With hands form into ball. Divide dough almost in half. Flatten larger portion slightly. Roll into 12-inch circle between 2 sheets waxed paper. Peel off top paper. Place dough in 9-inch pie pan, paper side up. Peel off paper; fit pastry loosely into pan. Fill as desired. Trim dough ½-inch beyond rim of pan. Roll out remaining dough between 2 sheets waxed paper. Place over filling. Peel off paper; cut slits to permit steam to escape. Trim ½-inch beyond rim of pan. Fold edges of both crusts under; seal and flute. Bake pie according to filling used.

VARIATIONS:

Apple Crescents

Follow recipe for Apple Pie. Use 2 recipes double crust pastry. Omit margarine. On lightly floured surface roll out pastry ¼ at a time to ⅛-inch thickness. Cut each ¼ into 3 (7-inch) circles. Place ½ cup filling on one-half of each circle. Fold dough over filling to form crescent. Seal edge with fork; cut slits in top. Place on cookie sheets. Bake in 425°F oven 15 minutes or until browned.
Makes 12

Apple Cranberry Pie

Follow recipe for Apple Pie. Increase corn starch to 2 tablespoons. Omit lemon juice. Toss 1 cup cranberries, halved, with apple slices. Turn into pastry-lined pie plate. Dot with margarine. Roll remaining pastry into 12-inch circle. Cut into 10 (½-inch) strips with pastry wheel or knife. Place 5 of the strips across filling. Weave lattice crust with remaining strips by folding back alternate strips as each cross strip is added. Fold trimmed edge of lower crusts over ends of strips; seal and flute. Sprinkle top of pastry lightly with sugar before baking. Bake in 400°F oven 15 minutes. Reduce heat to 350°F and bake 45 minutes longer or until bubbly and apples are tender.

Apple Blueberry Pie

Follow recipe for Apple Pie. Use 1¾ pounds apples (5 cups sliced). Increase corn starch to 3 tablespoons. Toss apples with 1 cup blueberries. Turn into pastry-lined pie plate. Dot with margarine. Continue as directed for Apple Pie.

To freeze uncooked pie: Follow recipe for Apple or Apple Cranberry Pie. Add 1 additional tablespoon corn starch to pie filling. Follow recipe cutting steam slits in pastry, as directed. (If frozen without slits, cutting frozen pie breaks pastry and frozen pie will have to be cooked slightly, then slits cut.) Wrap unbaked pie in plastic wrap or bag, foil or other moisture vapor-proof material. Seal with tape, label and freeze. Frozen unbaked pie may be held in freezer up to 4 months. Bake as directed in recipe for Apple or Apple Cranberry Pie, increasing time 15 to 20 minutes. If edge of pie begins to brown too much, cover with a strip of foil.

Fresh Lemon Meringue Pie

1½ cups sugar
¼ cup plus 2 Tbsp. cornstarch
¼ tsp. salt
½ cup cold water
½ cup fresh squeezed SUNKIST® Lemon juice
3 egg yolks, well beaten
2 Tbsp. butter or margarine
1½ cups boiling water
1 tsp. fresh grated SUNKIST® Lemon peel
Few drops yellow food coloring (optional)
1 (9-inch) baked pie shell
Meringue*

In saucepan, thoroughly combine sugar, cornstarch and salt. Gradually stir in cold water and lemon juice. Blend in egg yolks. Add butter and boiling water. Bring to boil over medium-high heat, stirring constantly. Reduce heat to medium and boil *1 minute*. Remove from heat; stir in lemon peel and food coloring. Pour into pie shell. Top with meringue, sealing well at edges. Bake at 350 degrees F. for 12 to 15 minutes. Cool 2 hours before serving.

Makes 6 to 8 servings

*Meringue

3 egg whites
¼ tsp. cream of tartar
6 Tbsp. sugar

Beat egg whites until foamy; add cream of tartar and continue beating to soft peak stage. Gradually add sugar, beating until egg whites are stiff, but not dry.

VARIATION:

For higher meringue use 4 egg whites, ¼ teaspoon cream of tartar and ½ cup sugar. Follow Meringue directions.

Lemon Light Yogurt Pie

Crust:
1⅔ cups finely crushed QUAKER® 100% Natural Cereal, original (about 2 cups cereal)
⅓ cup firmly packed brown sugar
¼ cup butter or margarine, melted

Filling:
1 envelope unflavored gelatin
⅓ cup plus 2 tablespoons granulated sugar
¼ teaspoon salt
2 eggs, separated
1 cup water
1 8-oz. carton (1 cup) lemon flavored yogurt

Heat oven to 350°F. For crust, combine all ingredients, mixing well. Reserve ¼ cup cereal mixture for topping; press remaining mixture onto bottom and side of greased 9-inch pie plate. Bake at 350°F. for 8 to 10 minutes or until golden brown. Press bottom and side of crust into place with spoon while still warm, if necessary. Cool. *(Continued)*

For filling, thoroughly mix gelatin, ⅓ cup sugar and salt in saucepan. Beat together egg yolks and water; stir into gelatin mixture. Cook over medium heat just until mixture comes to a boil, stirring constantly. Pour mixture into bowl; chill, stirring occasionally, until mixture mounds slightly when dropped from a spoon. Beat egg whites at medium speed on electric mixer until foamy. Beat at high speed while gradually adding remaining 2 tablespoons sugar, until stiff peaks form. Fold beaten egg whites and yogurt into gelatin mixture. Pour into prepared crust. Sprinkle with reserved cereal mixture; chill 3 to 4 hours or until firm. Garnish with lemon slices and mint leaves, if desired.

Makes 9-inch pie

Lemon Chiffon Pie
(Low Calorie/Low Fat)

1 envelope unflavored gelatin
¾ cup sugar, divided
½ cup water
¼ cup lemon juice
2 eggs, separated
1 packet BUTTER BUDS®
1 teaspoon grated lemon peel
1 8-inch Low-Sodium Pie Crust*
Lemon slices

In top of double boiler, combine gelatin and ½ cup sugar. Beat in water, lemon juice, and egg yolks. Heat, stirring constantly, until hot. Remove ½ cup of hot mixture to small bowl and slowly beat in BUTTER BUDS®, mixing well. Put BUTTER BUDS® mixture back into double boiler. Cook, stirring constantly, until mixture thickens and coats a metal spoon. Remove from heat and add lemon peel. Cool slightly. Chill until thickened but not firm. Beat egg whites until foamy; gradually add remaining sugar, beating until stiff. Fold egg whites into chilled gelatin mixture. Pour into 8-inch pie crust. Garnish with lemon slices. Chill several hours, until firm. By using BUTTER BUDS® instead of butter in this recipe, you have saved 94 calories and 35 mg cholesterol per serving.

Per Serving (⅛ of pie): Calories: 105; Fat: 1g

*Low-Sodium Pie Crust

1 cup sifted all-purpose flour
1 packet BUTTER BUDS®
¼ teaspoon cinnamon
⅛ teaspoon mace
1 teaspoon sesame seeds
2 tablespoons plus 1 teaspoon vegetable oil
2 to 3 tablespoons ice water

Blend flour with BUTTER BUDS®, cinnamon, mace, and sesame seeds. Add oil gradually, mixing into flour with a fork. When all of the oil has been added, work mixture lightly between fingertips until mixture is the size of small peas. Gradually add just enough ice water until dough is moist enough to hold together. Do not overwork dough. Form into a ball and roll out on floured surface with floured rolling pin, to a circle 1 inch larger than inverted 8- or 9-inch pie pan. Carefully transfer pastry to pie plate. Press dough into bottom and sides of pan, gently patting out air pockets. Preheat oven to 450°F. Prick bottom and sides of pastry with fork. Bake 8 to 10 minutes, or until lightly golden brown. Cool before using.

Per Serving (⅛ of crust): Calories: 95; Fat: 4g

Raspberry Paradise Pie

3 egg whites
¼ teaspoon baking powder
¼ teaspoon salt
¼ teaspoon cream of tartar
1 cup sugar
¾ cup 3-MINUTE BRAND® Oats
½ cup finely chopped walnuts
½ teaspoon vanilla
10-ounce package frozen raspberries, thawed
1 tablespoon cornstarch
Whipped Cream
Shredded Coconut

Beat egg whites with baking powder, salt and cream of tartar until nearly stiff. Add sugar gradually, beating until very stiff but not dry. Combine oats and walnuts and blend into egg whites. Fold in vanilla. Spoon into an 8 or 9-inch pie pan, making the meringue thicker around the edges, leaving a depression in the center for the filling. Bake at 325 degrees for 25 minutes, or until lightly browned. Cool.

Drain raspberries and place juice in a small saucepan. Carefully blend in cornstarch and cook over medium heat until juice is thickened. Cool slightly and then blend in the berries. Spoon mixture into the cooled meringue shell. Cover with whipped cream and garnish with coconut. Refrigerate several hours before serving.

NONE SUCH®

Traditional Mince Pie

1 (9-ounce) package JIFFY® Pie Crust Mix
1 (28-ounce) jar NONE SUCH® Ready-to-Use Mince Meat
1 egg yolk plus 2 tablespoons water, optional

Preheat oven to 425°; place rack in lower half of oven. Prepare pastry for 2-crust pie. Turn mince meat into pastry-lined 9-inch pie plate. Cover with top crust; cut slits near center. Seal and flute. For a more golden crust, mix egg yolk and water; brush over entire surface of pie. Bake 30 to 35 minutes or until golden brown.

Makes one 9-inch pie

VARIATIONS:

Peachy Mince Pie

Drain 1 (16-ounce) can sliced peaches. Turn mince meat into pastry shell; top with peaches. Proceed as above.

Mince Nut Pie

Stir together mince meat and 1 cup coarsely chopped nuts. Proceed as above.

Mince Apple Streusel Pie

Prepare pastry for 1-crust pie. Combine remaining pie crust mix, ¼ cup firmly packed brown sugar and 2 teaspoons ground cinnamon; cut in 2 tablespoons softened margarine or butter until crumbly. Stir in ¼ cup chopped nuts. Pare and slice 2 cooking apples; toss with 2 tablespoons flour. Arrange in pastry shell; top with mince meat, then streusel topping. Bake 25 to 30 minutes.

Cranberry Mince Pie

Stir together mince meat, 1 (14-ounce) jar cranberry-orange relish and 2 tablespoons flour. Proceed as above.

Mince Pie

4 medium apples, cored, pared and chopped (1 quart)
¾ cup sweet orange marmalade
½ cup dark seedless raisins
3 teaspoons KITCHEN BOUQUET®
1 teaspoon cinnamon
½ teaspoon cloves
⅛ teaspoon salt
½ cup chopped walnuts
1 tablespoon brandy (optional)
½ teaspoon vanilla
1 (9 inch) baked pie shell
½ cup flour
⅓ cup brown sugar (packed)
¼ cup butter

Combine apples, orange marmalade, raisins, KITCHEN BOUQUET, cinnamon, cloves and salt in saucepan. Bring to a boil. Reduce heat and simmer uncovered 10 minutes, stirring occasionally. Remove from heat. Stir in walnuts, brandy and vanilla. Turn into pie shell. Combine flour and sugar in mixing bowl. Mix in butter with fork or by pinching with fingertips until moist and crumbly. Sprinkle over pie. Bake in 400° oven for 20 minutes or until light golden brown on top. Serve warm or cool. Dollop with whipped cream, if desired. *Makes 1 (9 inch) pie*

Pumpkin Pie

1 9-inch unbaked pastry shell
1 cup brown sugar
2 tablespoons flour
½ teaspoon salt
¼ teaspoon cinnamon
¼ teaspoon nutmeg
1 cup cooked pumpkin
2 cups MILNOT®
2 eggs beaten
½ cup nut meats (optional)

Mix sugar, flour, salt and spices together and stir into pumpkin. Add MILNOT® and eggs. (Add nuts at this point, if used.) Pour into pie shell and bake at 450 degrees for 10 minutes; reduce heat to 350 degrees and continue baking for another 25 to 30 minutes, or until filling is firm (when knife inserted in pie comes out clean). Garnish with whipped MILNOT® Topping.

Whipping hints: To whip MILNOT® use clean, dry utensils. MILNOT® cannot be over-whipped. MILNOT® expands at least four times in volume when whipped.

Favorite Pumpkin Pie

Mix together 3 slightly beaten eggs, ¾ cup sugar, 2 to 3 teaspoons **FRENCH'S® Pumpkin Pie Spice**, ½ teaspoon salt, 1½ cups cooked or canned pumpkin, and 1 cup milk. Pour into 9-inch unbaked pie shell. Bake in 400°F. oven 45 to 50 minutes or until set.

Carnation® Pumpkin Pie

2 slightly beaten eggs
1½ cups canned pumpkin
1 cup sugar
½ teaspoon salt
1 teaspoon cinnamon
¼ teaspoon ginger
¼ teaspoon cloves
¼ teaspoon nutmeg
1⅔ cups *undiluted* **CARNATION® Evaporated Milk**
9-inch single-crust unbaked pie shell

Combine eggs, pumpkin, sugar, salt, and spices. Gradually add evaporated milk. Mix well. Pour into unbaked pie shell. Bake in hot oven (425°F.) 15 minutes; reduce to moderate oven (375°F.) and continue baking about 40 minutes, or until knife inserted near center of pie comes out clean. Cool before serving. Garnish, if desired. *Makes 9-inch pie*

Butter Crunchy Espresso Pie

Crust:
½ package pie crust mix
1 square (1 oz.) unsweetened chocolate, ground in rotary grater
¼ cup lumpfree light brown sugar
¾ cup finely chopped walnuts
1 teaspoon vanilla extract mixed with 1 tablespoon water

Start this pie as much as 2 days and at least 8 hours before serving: Stir together pie crust mix, grated chocolate, sugar and nuts with fork, eliminating lumps. Drizzle vanilla mixture over; stir and toss with fork as if making regular pastry. Fit a 12-inch square of aluminum foil into 9-inch oven glass pie plate, letting corners hang out. Line with pastry, pressing firmly in place. Bake in center of oven at 375°F. for 15 minutes. Cool. Freeze 45 to 60 minutes. Remove crust gently from plate; coax off aluminum foil. Return crust to plate. During this time, prepare filling.

Filling:
1 square (1 oz.) unsweetened chocolate, melted
1 stick (½ cup) softened butter
½ cup lumpfree light brown sugar
¼ cup granulated sugar
1 tablespoon instant **MEDAGLIA D'ORO® Espresso Coffee**
2 eggs

Cool chocolate. With portable electric mixer, beat butter until fluffy. Gradually beat in sugars and continue to beat 2 or 3 minutes. Scrape bowl occasionally. Add cooled chocolate and coffee; beat well. Add 1 egg at a time, beating 2 to 3 minutes after

each. Pour into prepared crust. Chill 5 or 6 hours, up to 2 days. Shortly before serving, prepare topping*

Serve in wedges to 8 to 10

*Topping

Whip together 1 cup heavy cream, 1 tablespoon instant **MEDAGLIA D'ORO® Espresso Coffee** and ¼ cup confectioners' sugar until soft standing peaks form. Use to decorate top of pie attractively. If desired, sprinkle with grated chocolate. Refrigerate.

Featherweight®
Chocolate Pie
(Low Calorie/Low Sodium)

1 baked 9-inch pie shell (or graham cracker crumb crust)
2 envelopes **FEATHERWEIGHT® Chocolate Pudding**
3 cups skim milk
1 envelope **FEATHERWEIGHT® Whipped Topping**

Place bottom of double boiler containing water on high heat. Place 3 cups skim milk in top of double boiler. Add contents of Chocolate Pudding envelopes. Mix well and stir until simmer point (185°-195°F.) is reached. Continue stirring for 3 minutes.

Pour pudding mixture into baked pie crust, saving back ½ cup, and chill until partially set.

Prepare: Whipped Topping as directed on package.

Blend: 1 cup of Whipped Topping into remaining ½ cup of pudding. Pour into partially set pie. Chill until set (about 4 hours) then garnish with remaining Whipped Topping.

Approx.	Calories	Protein (Grams)	Fat (Grams)	Carbohydrate Grams	Sodium (Mgs)
⅛ section of pie with pastry crust-					
	165	5	8	18	195
With graham cracker crumb crust-					
	180	4	7	24	215

Fudge Chiffon Pie

9-inch baked pastry shell or crumb crust
1 envelope unflavored gelatine
¼ cup cold water
¾ cup boiling water
⅛ teaspoon salt
3-ounce package cream cheese
1½ cups (1-lb. can) **HERSHEY'S® Chocolate Fudge Topping**
3 egg whites
2 tablespoons sugar

Prepare pastry shell or crumb crust; set aside. Sprinkle gelatine onto cold water in a small bowl; allow to soften. Add boiling water and salt; stir until dissolved. In small mixer bowl beat cream cheese until smooth; add fudge topping beating until well blended. Gradually add gelatine mixture; chill until set.

In another small mixer bowl beat egg whites with sugar until stiff peaks form. Beat chocolate mixture until smooth; carefully fold in egg whites. Pour into pastry shell, crumb crust or chocolate cups. Chill thoroughly. Garnish with sweetened whipped cream or dessert topping and fresh fruit, if desired.

Chocolate-Chiffon Pie

1 envelope unflavored gelatin
½ cup cold water
3 1-oz. squares unsweetened chocolate
1 cup **MARSHMALLOW FLUFF®**
½ cup milk
2 egg yolks, slightly beatened
½ tsp. vanilla extract
2 egg whites, at room temperature, beaten until stiff
½ cup heavy or whipping cream
1 graham cracker-crumb crust
¼ cup chopped nuts

In medium saucepan combine gelatin and water; let stand 1 minute. Over low heat, heat, stirring constantly, until gelatin is completely dissolved. Melt chocolate in double-boiler and stir in **FLUFF®** and milk. Add egg yolks and vanilla; mix well. Add dissolved gelatin. Chill. When thickened to the consistency of unbeaten egg whites, beat with mixer until foamy. Fold in beaten egg whites. Beat heavy or whipping cream until soft peaks form. Fold into chiffon mixture. Turn into pie crust. Sprinkle with nuts and chill until set. *Makes 6-8 servings*

Tia Maria
Black Bottom Pie

1½ envelopes unflavored gelatin
250 mL or 1 cup sugar, divided
10 mL or 1¼ tablespoons cornstarch
4 eggs, separated
500 mL or 2 cups scalded milk
2 squares unsweetened chocolate, melted
5 mL or 1 teaspoon vanilla
1 9-inch pie shell
75 mL or ⅓ cup **TIA MARIA®** liqueur
1.25 mL or ¼ teaspoon cream of tartar
Grated semi-sweet chocolate

Prepare the pie crust and cook until done but not browned. Mix gelatin, 125 mL or ½ cup of the sugar, and cornstarch in the top of a double boiler. Beat egg yolks and milk; add to gelatin mixture and cook over boiling water, stirring constantly until mixture coats spoon. Divide custard in half. To one part add melted chocolate and vanilla; mix well and turn into pie shell. Chill until firm. To second part add **TIA MARIA®** and chill until it starts to thicken. Beat egg whites with cream of tartar until frothy. Gradually add remaining sugar and continue beating until egg whites hold their shape. Fold in chilled custard and turn onto chocolate layer. Garnish with whipped cream, top with grated chocolate and chill.

Chocolate Pie
With Pretzel Crust

1 13-ounce package **ROLD GOLD®** Brand Pretzels
3 tablespoons sugar
½ cup butter or margarine, melted

Crush pretzels very fine in blender or between waxed paper. Add sugar and butter or margarine. Mix thoroughly. Press ½ of mixture in 9″ pie plate. Bake at 350°F. for 8 minutes. Cool.
    Pour in CHOCOLATE FILLING* and top with remaining pretzel mixture. Chill.

*Chocolate Filling

⅔ cup sugar
4 tablespoons cornstarch
2½ cups milk
3 3-ounce squares unsweetened chocolate, cut in small pieces
3 egg yolks, slightly beaten
1 teaspoon vanilla extract

Combine sugar, cornstarch, milk and chocolate in top of double boiler. Cook over boiling water until thickened, stirring constantly. Cover and cook 15 minutes. Stir part of hot chocolate mixture into egg yolks. Add to chocolate mixture. Mix thoroughly. Cool. Add vanilla extract and mix thoroughly.

Tom's® Peanut Crunch Pie

1 unbaked 9-inch pastry shell
¼ cup sugar
1 tablespoon quick-cooking tapioca
¼ teaspoon salt
1 cup dark corn syrup
¼ cup water
3 eggs
½ teaspoon vanilla
2 tablespoons butter or margarine
1 cup **TOM'S®** Toasted Peanuts, coarsely chopped

Prepare pastry shell but do not bake. Blend sugar, tapioca, and salt in a medium-size saucepan. Stir in corn syrup and water. Bring to a boil, stirring constantly. Boil 4 minutes. Beat eggs slightly in a bowl. Pour hot syrup slowly into eggs, stirring vigorously. Stir in vanilla and butter. Cool. Scatter chopped peanuts over bottom of pastry shell. Add cooled pie filling. Bake in a hot oven (450°F.) for 8 minutes. Reduce heat to moderately low (325° F.) and bake for 25 to 35 minutes, or until a silver knife inserted in the center comes out clean. Serve warm, or cool and top with sweetened whipped cream.

Grasshopper Pie

3 tablespoons melted butter (or margarine)
21 chocolate wafers, crushed
36 marshmallows
¾ cup milk
5 tablespoons **ARROW®** Creme de Menthe
2 tablespoons **ARROW®** White Creme de Cacao
1½ cups heavy cream

In medium bowl, combine butter and crushed wafers. Press crumb mixture on bottom and up sides of 9 inch pie plate. Bake 5 minutes in preheated 375°F. oven. Cool. In 2 quart saucepan, melt marshmallows in milk over low heat, stirring constantly. Mix in liqueurs. Cool until slightly thickened. Beat cream until it mounds slightly. Fold into marshmallow mixture. Pour into pie shell. Freeze. Garnish with whipped cream and mint leaves, if desired.
Serves 8

Nestlé

Tangy Butterscotch Lemon Pie

1 cup boiling water
1 3-oz. pkg. lemon flavor gelatin
¼ measuring teaspoon salt
3 eggs
1 6-oz. pkg. (1 cup) **NESTLÉ Butterscotch Morsels**
1 9″ prepared graham cracker pie shell
Whipped cream

In small bowl, combine boiling water, gelatin and salt; stir until gelatin is dissolved; set aside. In blender container, process eggs at medium speed for 2 minutes. Add **NESTLÉ Butterscotch Morsels** and lemon gelatin mixture; blend until smooth. Set aside about 5 minutes; pour into prepared pie shell. Chill about 2 hours or until firm. Garnish with whipped cream.

Makes one 9″ pie

NONE SUCH®

Ambrosia Pie

1 (9-inch) unbaked pastry shell
1 (9-ounce) package **NONE SUCH® Condensed Mincemeat**
1 cup water
2 eggs, beaten
1 (16-ounce) container **BORDEN® Sour Cream**
2 tablespoons sugar
1 teaspoon vanilla extract
2 tablespoons chopped nuts

Preheat oven to 425°. In small saucepan, break mincemeat into small pieces; add water. Boil briskly 1 minute. Cool. Pour mincemeat into pastry shell. Bake 20 minutes. In small bowl, combine eggs, sour cream, sugar and vanilla. Pour over mincemeat; sprinkle with nuts. Return to oven 8 to 10 minutes or until sour cream mixture is set. Cool. Chill thoroughly before serving. Refrigerate leftovers. *Makes one 9-inch pie*

Uncle Ben's®

Fantasy Rice Pie

1½ cups cottage cheese
½ cup milk
1 package (3¾ ounces) lemon instant pudding and pie filling
1½ cups chilled, cooked **UNCLE BEN'S® CONVERTED® Brand Rice**
1 (8 or 9-inch) graham cracker pie crust
½ cup sour cream
Fresh strawberry slices or other fruit for garnish

Beat cottage cheese using an electric mixer until fairly smooth. Add milk and pudding mix; beat until well blended. Stir in rice. Spoon into prepared crust. Chill. Spread sour cream over top before serving. Garnish with fruit. *Makes 6 servings*

Piña Colada Ribbon Pie

1 box (8½ ounces) chocolate wafers, finely crushed
¼ cup butter or margarine, melted
1 can (16 ounces) crushed pineapple, with juice
5 teaspoons cornstarch
⅔ cup plus 1 tablespoon **CocoRibe® Coconut Rum Liqueur**, divided
1 quart vanilla ice cream, softened slightly
1 cup (½ pint) heavy cream

In small bowl, mix wafer crumbs with melted butter. Reserve 2 tablespoons crumb mixture. Press remaining crumb mixture into a 9-inch pie plate. Freeze 30 minutes.

Measure 2 tablespoons pineapple juice from crushed pineapple. In small cup, blend pineapple juice with cornstarch. In saucepan, combine pineapple and juice and cornstarch mixture. Bring to a boil, stirring constantly; cook 1 minute. Remove from heat, stir in ⅔ cup liqueur; chill in refrigerator.

Spread 2 cups softened ice cream in prepared pie shell. Return to freezer for 30 minutes. Spread half of the pineapple mixture over top of frozen ice cream, return to freezer for 30 minutes. Repeat layering process with ice cream and pineapple filling. Before serving, combine remaining 1 tablespoon liqueur with heavy cream. Beat until soft peaks form. Decorate pie with whipped cream, sprinkle with reserved crumbs. Slice with warm knife. *Yield: 10 servings*

Note: For easier slicing, pie should be tempered at room temperature for 15 minutes. Or, placed in refrigerator for 30 minutes.

Eggnog Custard Pie

In saucepan, stir 1 envelope unflavored gelatin into 1½ cups commercial eggnog; heat to scalding. (OR **micro-cook** on High 3½-4 minutes to 160°F.) "Melt" 1 can **THANK YOU® BRAND Egg Custard** according to directions on label. Combine Egg Custard and eggnog.* Pour into a cool 9-inch crumb crust (either chocolate or graham cracker). Chill 3 hours or until set. Decorate with whipped cream, chocolate curls, and red cherries. Or simply sprinkle with nutmeg.

*For a "spirited" dessert, add 2-3 teaspoons rum at this point.

JELL-O®

Dream Pie

2 envelopes **DREAM WHIP® Whipped Topping Mix**
2¾ cups cold milk
2 packages (4-serving size) **JELL-O® Brand Instant Pudding & Pie Filling**, any flavor
1 baked 9-inch pie shell, cooled

Prepare whipped topping mix with 1 cup of the milk as directed on package, using large mixer bowl. Add remaining 1¾ cups milk and the pie filling mix. Blend; then beat at high speed for 2 minutes, scraping bowl occasionally. Spoon into pie shell. Chill at least 4 hours.

Domino®

No-Bake Fresh Fruit Tart

8 ozs. cream cheese, softened
1 tablespoon grated orange rind
2 tablespoons orange juice
½ cup **DOMINO® Confectioners 10-X Powdered Sugar**
8-inch ready-to-fill crumb crust or 6 individual crumb tart shells (bought)
2 to 3 cups fresh whole berries, seedless green grapes, pitted sweet cherries, sliced peaches, nectarines, plums, etc.

Beat cheese, rind, juice, and sugar together until fluffy. Fill pie crust or tart shells with cheese mixture. Chill thoroughly. Top with fruit. Add 1 tablespoon lemon juice to peaches or nectarines to prevent discoloration. Sift more sugar generously over fruit.

Yields 6 servings

Note: For an especially festive tart, stand berries with tips up, or use circles of different fruits. Green grapes, strawberries, and blueberries make a festive combination.

VARIATION:

Busy Cooks' Dessert

A simple crustless version of the No-Bake Fresh Fruit Tart. Mix the cheese, rind, 4 tablespoons juice, and sugar as directed. Keep at room temperature. Arrange one or more fruits in dessert dishes, chill. At serving time sprinkle fruit with more sugar and top with cheese sauce. Garnish with grated orange rind if desired.

Chocolate Crumb Crust

1½ cups of **MALT-O-MEAL® Puffed Rice Cereal**
1 package (6 oz.) semi-sweet chocolate morsels
¼ cup of butter
½ cup toasted coconut

Place cereal in a shallow baking dish and bake in 350° oven for 10 minutes; chop coarsely. Combine chocolate morsels and butter; cook over very low heat, stirring constantly until chocolate is melted. Blend cereal and coconut into melted chocolate. Press firmly and evenly against bottom and sides of a 9 inch pie pan. Chill before filling with your favorite pudding or ice cream.

Makes one 9 inch chocolate crust

Brownies

Princess Brownies

1 pkg. family size brownie mix
1 8-oz. pkg. **PHILADELPHIA BRAND Cream Cheese**
⅓ cup sugar
1 egg
½ teaspoon vanilla

Prepare brownie mix as directed on package. Combine softened cream cheese and sugar; mix until well blended. Stir in egg and vanilla. Spread half of brownie batter onto bottom of greased

13 × 9-inch baking pan. Cover with cream cheese mixture; spoon on remaining brownie batter. Cut through batter with knife several times for marble effect. Bake at 350°, 35 to 40 minutes or until wooden pick inserted in center comes out clean. Cool; cut into squares.

Double Chocolate Brownies

½ cup butter or margarine
¾ cup sugar
1 egg
½ cup sour cream
1 teaspoon vanilla
1 cup unsifted all-purpose flour
¼ cup **HERSHEY'S® Unsweetened Cocoa**
¼ teaspoon baking soda
¼ teaspoon salt
1 cup **HERSHEY'S® Semi-Sweet Chocolate Mini Chips**
Easy Brownie Frosting*

Cream butter or margarine, sugar and egg in small mixer bowl until fluffy. Add sour cream and vanilla; beat well. Combine flour, cocoa, baking soda and salt; blend into creamed mixture. Stir in **Mini Chips**. Spread batter evenly in greased 9-inch square baking pan. Bake at 350° for 30 to 35 minutes or until toothpick inserted in center barely comes out clean. Do not overbake. Cool. Frost with Easy Brownie Frosting. Sprinkle with additional Mini Chips or walnut halves. Cut into squares. *20 brownies*

*Easy Brownie Frosting

3 tablespoons butter, softened
3 tablespoons **HERSHEY'S® Unsweetened Cocoa**
½ teaspoon vanilla
1¼ cups confectioners' sugar
2 tablespoons milk

Cream butter and cocoa in small mixer bowl; add vanilla and confectioners' sugar. Blend in milk; beat until mixture reaches spreading consistency. *About 1 cup*

Peanut Fudge Brownies

¾ cup (1½ sticks) butter
1½ cups granulated sugar
1½ teaspoons vanilla
3 eggs
1½ cups all-purpose flour
½ cup unsweetened cocoa
½ teaspoon each: baking powder, salt
1 square (1 ounce) unsweetened chocolate
1½ tablespoons each: butter, creamy peanut butter
1 cup confectioners' sugar
2 to 3 tablespoons hot tap water
2 **CLARK® Bars** (1.75 ounces each), coarsely chopped

In saucepan, melt butter; cool slightly. Blend in granulated sugar and vanilla. Beat in eggs, one at a time. Combine flour, cocoa, baking powder and salt. Add to butter mixture; mix well. Pour into greased 13 × 2-inch pan. Bake at 350° for 25 to 30 minutes. Cool on rack. In saucepan over low heat, melt chocolate, butter and peanut butter. Remove from heat. Blend in confectioners' sugar and enough hot water to make a pourable glaze. Pour over brownies, spreading evenly with spatula. Sprinkle crushed **CLARK® Bars** over top. When glaze has set, cut into bars.   *3 dozen*

Nestlé
Frosted Fudgie Brownies

Brownies:
1 cup sugar
2 eggs
½ cup butter, softened
2 envelopes (2-oz.) **NESTLÉ CHOCO-BAKE**
1 measuring teaspoon vanilla extract
⅔ cup *unsifted* flour
½ measuring teaspoon baking powder
½ measuring teaspoon salt
½ cup chopped nuts

Fudge Frosting:
1 egg yolk
2 measuring tablespoons butter, melted
1 envelope (1-oz.) **NESTLÉ CHOCO-BAKE**
1 measuring teaspoon milk
½ measuring teaspoon vanilla extract
1 cup sifted confectioners' sugar

BROWNIES:
Preheat oven to 350°F. In small bowl, combine sugar, eggs, butter, **NESTLÉ CHOCO-BAKE** and vanilla extract; beat until creamy. Add flour, baking powder and salt; mix well. Add nuts. Spread into greased 8″ square baking pan. Bake at 350°F. for 30 minutes.
Cool completely. Spread with Fudge Frosting. Cut into 2″ squares.

FUDGE FROSTING:
In small bowl, combine egg yolk, butter, **NESTLÉ CHOCO-BAKE**, milk and vanilla extract; mix until well blended. Gradually add confectioners' sugar; beat until creamy.
Makes: sixteen 2″ squares and ¾ cup frosting

Saucepan Brownies

½ cup sugar
2 tablespoons butter
2 tablespoons water
1⅓ cups **HERSHEY'S® Semi-Sweet Chocolate Mini Chips**
2 eggs
⅔ cup unsifted all-purpose flour
¼ teaspoon baking soda
¼ teaspoon salt
1 teaspoon vanilla
¾ cup chopped nuts (optional)

Combine sugar, butter and water in saucepan. Cook over medium heat, stirring occasionally, until mixture boils. Remove from heat; add Mini Chips stirring until melted. Add eggs; beat with spoon until well blended. Combine flour, baking soda and salt; stir into chocolate mixture. Stir in vanilla and chopped nuts; pour into greased 8 or 9-inch square pan. Bake at 325° for 25 to 30 minutes or until toothpick inserted in center barely comes out clean. Do not overbake. Cool; sprinkle with confectioners' sugar or frost as desired. Cut into squares.   *20 brownies*

Bars

Good

100% PURE MinuteMaid®
Tangy Lemon Squares

1 cup (½ lb.) butter or margarine, softened
½ cup powdered sugar (unsifted)
2⅓ cups all-purpose flour (unsifted)
4 eggs
2 cups granulated sugar
⅓ cup **MINUTE MAID® 100% Pure Lemon Juice**
1 teaspoon baking powder
About 2 tablespoons powdered sugar

In a large bowl, cream together butter and the ½ cup powdered sugar until fluffy. Add 2 cups of the flour, beating until blended. Spread evenly over the bottom of a well-greased 9 by 13-inch baking pan. Bake in a preheated 350°F. oven for 20 minutes.
    Meanwhile, in a small mixing bowl beat the eggs until light and foamy. Gradually add granulated sugar, beating until thick and blended. Add lemon juice, remaining ⅓ cup flour, and baking powder; beat until thoroughly blended. Pour lemon mixture over baked crust and return to oven; bake 25 to 30 minutes until golden and custard is set. Remove from oven and sprinkle evenly with powdered sugar; let cool. To serve, cut in small squares or bars.
Makes about 20 pieces

SKIPPY®
Orange Peanut Butter Bars

1 cup **SKIPPY® Creamy or Chunk Style Peanut Butter**
⅔ cup **MAZOLA®/NUCOA® Margarine**
1 teaspoon vanilla
1½ cups firmly packed light brown sugar
3 eggs
1¼ cups unsifted flour
½ teaspoon salt
¾ cup sifted confectioners sugar
1 teaspoon grated orange rind
4 teaspoons orange juice

Grease 13 × 9 × 2-inch baking pan. Mix together peanut butter, margarine and vanilla in large bowl; beat with electric mixer on medium speed until well blended. Beat in sugar until light and fluffy. Beat in eggs, 1 at a time. Stir in flour and salt just until well blended. Spread batter in prepared pan. Bake in 350°F. (moderate) oven about 30 minutes or until center springs back when lightly touched. Remove from oven. Cool slightly on wire rack. Stir together confectioners' sugar, orange rind and juice until smooth. Drizzle orange glaze over warm cookies in pan; swirl with bowl of spoon to make a random pattern. Cut into 36 (3 × 1-inch) bars.

VARIATION:
Chocolate Swirl Topping

Follow recipe for Orange Peanut Butter Bars as directed. Melt ¼ cup semisweet chocolate pieces with 1 tablespoon **MAZOLA®/ NUCOA® Margarine** over simmering water in top of double boiler. Drizzle over the orange glaze for a black and orange pattern. When cool, cut into bars.

EAGLE® BRAND
Magic Cookie Bars

½ cup margarine or butter
1½ cups graham cracker crumbs
1 (14-ounce) can **EAGLE® Brand Sweetened Condensed Milk** (not evaporated milk)
1 (6-ounce) package semi-sweet chocolate morsels
1 (3½-ounce) can flaked coconut (1⅓ cups)
1 cup chopped nuts

Preheat oven to 350°F. (325°F. for glass dish). In 13 × 9-inch baking pan, melt margarine in oven. Sprinkle crumbs over margarine; pour **EAGLE® Brand** evenly over crumbs. Top evenly with remaining ingredients; press down firmly. Bake 25 to 30 minutes or until lightly browned. Cool thoroughly before cutting. Store loosely covered at room temperature. *Makes 24 bars*

VARIATIONS:

Apricot Bars

Substitute 1 (6-ounce) package dried apricots, chopped, (1 cup) for chocolate morsels. Proceed as directed.

Butterscotch Bars

Substitute 1 (6-ounce) package butterscotch-flavored morsels for chocolate morsels. Proceed as directed.

Confetti Bars

Substitute 1 cup plain multi-colored candy-coated chocolate pieces for chocolate morsels. Proceed as directed.

Raisin Bars

Substitute wheat germ for graham cracker crumbs. Substitute 1 cup seedless raisins for chocolate morsels. Proceed as directed.

 Ralston Purina Company

Apricot Bars

Filling:
1 package (6 oz.) dried apricots
½ teaspoon cinnamon
⅛ teaspoon ground cloves
⅔ cup packed brown sugar

Crumb Mixture:
½ cup butter or margarine, softened
¾ cup packed brown sugar
1¼ cups all-purpose flour*
¼ teaspoon salt
¼ teaspoon baking soda
¾ cup **Instant** or **Regular RALSTON®**

FILLING:
In 1-quart saucepan combine apricots and spices. Add just enough water to cover. Simmer, covered, 15 minutes or until tender. Drain. Mash apricots with fork. Add sugar. Mix thoroughly. Cool.

CRUMB MIXTURE:
Preheat oven to 400°. Butter 9-inch square baking pan. Cream together butter and sugar. Stir together remaining ingredients. Add to

creamed mixture. Mix well to form coarse crumbs. Pack ⅔ of crumb mixture into pan. Spread with cooled filling. Sprinkle with remaining crumbs. Pack lightly. Bake about 20 minutes or until top is lightly browned. Cool. Cut into bars. For a delicious dessert, cut into larger pieces and top with ice cream. *Makes 24*

Stir flour; then spoon into measuring cups.

Orangeola Bars

1¼ cups (about ⅓ package) **HEALTH VALLEY® ORANGEOLA® Cereal**
¼ cup **HEALTH VALLEY® SPROUTS 7™ Cereal**
⅓ cup finely ground walnuts or pecans
2 tablespoons fresh or dried grated coconut
Dash of nutmeg
2 tablespoons **HEALTH VALLEY® Clover Honey**
½ teaspoon vanilla
2 egg whites, beaten stiff

Preheat oven to 275°F. and butter a 6½ × 11 × 2-inch baking pan. In a mixing bowl, combine **ORANGEOLA®**, **SPROUTS 7™**, nuts, coconut and nutmeg. Add honey and vanilla and mix thoroughly (it might be necessary to use your hands to do this). Then fold in egg whites and allow mixture to stand 2 to 3 minutes. Spread or press into prepared pan and bake in preheated oven for 20 minutes. Remove from oven, cut into 20 or 24 bars and transfer immediately to glass or china plate to cool.

Yield: 20 or 24 bars

Golden Meringue Dessert Bars

Crust:
⅔ cup butter, softened
⅓ cup light brown sugar, packed
2 egg yolks
1 teaspoon vanilla
1½ cups flour

Filling:
1 can (1 lb., 4 oz.) **DOLE® Crushed Pineapple**
1 cup dried apricots, cut up
½ cup sugar
3 tablespoons cornstarch
1 teaspoon grated orange peel
¼ teaspoon ground nutmeg

Orange Meringue:
3 egg whites
¼ teaspoon cream of tartar
⅔ cup sugar
½ teaspoon grated orange peel

CRUST:
Beat butter and brown sugar until light and fluffy. Beat in egg yolks and vanilla. Fold in flour until blended. Pat into a 9-inch square glass baking pan. Bake in a preheated 350° F. oven 15 minutes until lightly browned. Place on wire rack to cool.

(Continued)

FILLING:

Drain pineapple, reserving all syrup. Pour syrup over apricots in a small saucepan. Cook over medium heat, stirring occasionally for about ½ hour until all liquid is absorbed. Stir in sugar, pineapple, cornstarch, orange peel and nutmeg. Cook stirring constantly until mixture boils and becomes clear. (This will be very thick) Remove from heat and cool slightly. Spread over crust.

ORANGE MERINGUE:

Beat egg whites to soft peaks. Add cream of tartar and beat in sugar gradually until stiff peaks form. Beat in orange peel. Spread over warm filling.

Bake in a 350° F. oven 18 to 20 minutes until golden. Cool before cutting. *Makes 16 bars*

Land O' Lakes Lemon-Butter Snowbars

Crust:

½ cup **LAND O LAKES® Sweet Cream Butter**, softened
1½ cup all-purpose flour
¼ cup sugar

Filling:

2 eggs
¾ cup sugar
2 Tbsp. all-purpose flour
¼ tsp. baking powder
3 Tbsp. lemon juice

Confectioners' sugar

Preheat Oven: 350°. In 1½-qt. mixer bowl combine crust ingredients; mix at low speed until blended (1 min.). Pat into ungreased 8″ sq. baking pan. Bake near center of 350° oven for 15 to 20 min. or until brown on edges. Meanwhile, prepare filling; pour filling over partially baked crust. Return to oven for 18 to 20 min. or until set. Sprinkle with confectioners' sugar. Cool.

FILLING:

In 1½-qt. mixing bowl combine all filling ingredients; blend well.
Yield: 16 bars

Orange Flavor Coconut Chews

1 cup unsifted all-purpose flour
1 teaspoon **CALUMET® Baking Powder**
½ teaspoon salt
¼ cup butter or margarine
1 cup sugar
2 tablespoons **TANG™ Orange Flavor Instant Breakfast Drink**
1 egg
2 tablespoons water
1⅓ cups (about) **BAKER'S® ANGEL FLAKE® Coconut**
1 square **BAKER'S® Semi-Sweet Chocolate**, melted (optional)

Mix flour with baking powder and salt. Cream butter. Combine sugar and instant breakfast drink; gradually blend into butter. Add egg and water and beat until smooth. Fold in flour mixture; stir in coconut. Spread batter in greased 8-inch square pan. Bake at 350° for 35 to 40 minutes, or until cake begins to pull away from sides of pan. Cool in pan. Drizzle with melted chocolate. Let stand until firm; then cut into squares or bars. *Makes about 20 cookies*

Crumb Top Choco-Peanut Butter Bars

⅔ cup **PETER PAN® Peanut Butter, Creamy**
6 ounces (1 cup) semi-sweet chocolate pieces
1½ cups quick oats, uncooked
1¼ cups flour
½ teaspoon baking soda
½ teaspoon salt
1 stick (½ cup) butter, softened
1 cup packed brown sugar
1 egg
1 teaspoon vanilla

Grease a 13 by 9 by 2-inch pan. Over hot, not boiling, water melt the chocolate pieces. In a small bowl combine the oats, flour, baking soda and salt. In a large bowl combine and blend until creamy the butter, brown sugar and peanut butter. Add the egg and vanilla and mix well. Gradually add the flour-oat mixture and beat until well mixed. Pour ¾ of the dough into a greased baking pan. Spread with melted chocolate. Then dot chocolate with remaining dough. Bake in 350°F. oven 25 minutes. When slightly cooled, cut into 2 by 1-inch bars. *Yield: 48 bars, 2 by 1 inch*

Best Foods®
HELLMANN'S®

Chocolate Cheesecake Bars

1 package (18½ oz.) chocolate cake mix
½ cup **BEST FOODS®/HELLMANN'S® Real Mayonnaise**
12 ounces cream cheese, softened
½ cup sugar
2 eggs
1 package (6 oz) semisweet chocolate pieces, melted
1 teaspoon vanilla

In large bowl stir together cake mix and **REAL MAYONNAISE** until coarse crumbs form. Press evenly onto bottom and up sides of 15½ × 10½ × 1-inch jelly roll pan. In large bowl with mixer at medium speed beat cream cheese until smooth. Gradually beat in sugar. Add eggs, one at a time, beating well after each. Beat in chocolate and vanilla until smooth. Spread evenly over crust. Bake in 350°F oven 30 to 35 minutes or until set. Cool on wire rack. Refrigerate several hours. Cut into bars.
Makes 75 (1 × 2-inch) bars

Gold'n Honey Nut Crunch Bars

PAM® Vegetable Cooking Spray
⅓ cup **SUE BEE® Honey**
⅓ cup margarine or butter
1 cup packed brown sugar
½ teaspoon ground cinnamon, if desired
1 teaspoon vanilla
5 cups **GOLDEN GRAHAMS® Cereal**
1 cup **FISHER® Mixed Nuts** or **Peanuts**

Spray square pan, 9 × 9 × 2 inches, with **PAM® Vegetable Cooking Spray**. Heat honey, margarine, brown sugar and cinnamon to boiling in 3-quart saucepan; boil 2 minutes. Remove from heat; stir in vanilla. Gradually fold in cereal until completely coated. Fold in nuts. Press cereal mixture in pan with a piece of waxed paper. Let stand at least 1 hour. Cut into bars, about 2¼ × 1½ inches. *24 bars*

Cookies

Chocolate Scotcheroos

1 cup light corn syrup
1 cup sugar
1 cup peanut butter
6 cups **KELLOGG'S® RICE KRISPIES® Cereal**
1 pkg. (6 oz., 1 cup) semi-sweet chocolate morsels
1 pkg. (6 oz., 1 cup) butterscotch morsels

1. Measure corn syrup and sugar into large saucepan. Cook over medium heat, stirring frequently, until sugar dissolves and mixture begins to boil. Remove from heat. Stir in peanut butter. Mix well. Add **KELLOGG'S® RICE KRISPIES® Cereal**. Stir until well coated. Press mixture into buttered 13 × 9 × 2-inch pan. Set aside.
2. Melt chocolate and butterscotch morsels together in small saucepan over low heat, stirring constantly. Spread evenly over cereal mixture. Let stand until firm. Cut into 1 × 2-inch bars to serve. *Yield: 48 bars*

® Kellogg Company

Crispie Treats

4 cups miniature marshmallows
¼ cup margarine
½ cup peanut butter
⅛ teaspoon salt
4 cups crisp rice cereal
1½ cups **"M&M'S" Plain** or **Peanut Chocolate Candies**

Melt together marshmallows, margarine, peanut butter and salt in heavy saucepan over low heat, stirring occasionally, until smooth. Pour over combined cereal and candies, tossing lightly until thor-

oughly coated. With greased fingers, gently shape into 1½-inch balls. Place on waxed paper; cool at room temperature until set.
Makes about 3 dozen cookies

VARIATION:

After cereal mixture is thoroughly coated, press lightly into greased 13 × 9-inch baking pan. Cool thoroughly; cut into bars.
Makes one 13 × 9-inch pan of bars

Nestlé

Toll House® Cookies

2¼ cups *unsifted* flour
1 measuring teaspoon baking soda
1 measuring teaspoon salt
1 cup butter, softened
¾ cup sugar
¾ cup firmly packed brown sugar
1 measuring teaspoon vanilla extract
2 eggs
One 12-oz. pkg. (2 cups) **NESTLÉ Semi-Sweet Real Chocolate Morsels**
1 cup chopped nuts

Preheat oven to 375°F. In small bowl, combine flour, baking soda and salt; set aside. In large bowl, combine butter, sugar, brown sugar and vanilla extract; beat until creamy. Beat in eggs. Gradually add flour mixture; mix well. Stir in **NESTLÉ Semi-Sweet Real Chocolate Morsels** and nuts. Drop by rounded measuring teaspoonfuls onto ungreased cookie sheets. Bake at 375°F. 8-10 minutes. *Makes: One hundred 2" cookies*

VARIATION:

Toll House® Pan Cookies

To make quick **Toll House®** Pan Cookies, spread the original **Toll House®** Cookie dough into a greased 15" × 10" × 1" baking pan. Bake at 375°F for just 20 minutes. Cool; cut into thirty-five 2" squares.

Polka Dot Peanut Butter Jumbos

1 cup margarine
1 cup peanut butter
1 cup granulated sugar
1 cup firmly packed brown sugar
2 eggs
2 cups flour
1 teaspoon soda
1½ cups **"M&M'S" Plain** or **Peanut Chocolate Candies**

Beat together margarine, peanut butter and sugars until light and fluffy; blend in eggs. Add combined flour and soda; mix well. Stir in candies. Drop dough by level ¼ cup measure onto greased cookie sheet about 3 inches apart. Bake at 350°F. for 14 to 15 minutes or until edges are golden brown. Cool on cookie sheet 3 minutes; remove to wire rack to cool thoroughly.
Makes about 2 dozen 4-inch cookies

VARIATION:

For 2½-inch cookies, drop dough by rounded tablespoonfuls onto greased cookie sheet. Bake at 350°F. for 12 to 13 minutes.
Makes about 4 dozen cookies

Sierra Nuggets • Country Style Chocolate Chip Cookies

1 cup butter (softened)
1 cup brown sugar
1½ cups white sugar
1 Tbsp. milk
1½ tsp. vanilla
2 eggs
1 cup fresh corn flakes (crumbled)
3 cups oatmeal
1½ cups flour
1¼ tsp. baking soda
½ tsp. mace
1 tsp. salt
1½ tsp. cinnamon
¼ tsp. nutmeg
⅛ tsp. powdered cloves
4 oz. coconut
1 pkg. (2 cups) **GUITTARD® Chocolate Drops**
1 cup walnuts or pine nuts (chopped)

Preheat oven to 350°. Cream together butter and sugars. Add milk and vanilla. Beat in eggs. Stir in cornflakes and oatmeal. Sift together flour, baking soda, mace, salt, cinnamon, nutmeg and cloves. Add to mixture and mix thoroughly. Stir in coconut, chocolate and nuts. Drop by well rounded teaspoon onto greased cookie sheets. Bake 10 minutes at 350°.

Yield: Approx. 8 dozen

Macaroon Kiss Cookies

⅓ cup butter or margarine
1 package (3 ounces) cream cheese, softened
¾ cup sugar
1 egg yolk
2 teaspoons almond extract
2 teaspoons orange juice
1¼ cups unsifted all-purpose flour
2 teaspoons baking powder
¼ teaspoon salt
5 cups (14-ounce package) flaked coconut
1 9-ounce package **HERSHEY'S® Milk Chocolate Kisses** (about 54)

Cream butter or margarine, cream cheese and sugar until light and fluffy. Add egg yolk, almond extract and orange juice; beat well. Combine flour, baking powder and salt; gradually add to creamed mixture until well blended. Stir in 3 cups flaked coconut. Cover dough and chill about 1 hour. Shape dough into 1-inch balls. Roll balls in remaining coconut; place on ungreased cookie sheet. Bake at 350° for 10 to 12 minutes or until lightly browned on bottom. Remove from oven and press a milk chocolate kiss into center of each cookie. Allow to cool one minute. Carefully remove cookies from sheet and cool until chocolate kiss is firm.

About 4½ dozen cookies

Peanut Butter Piece Cookies

⅔ cup butter or margarine
1 cup sugar
1 egg
1½ teaspoons vanilla
1⅔ cups unsifted all-purpose flour
½ cup unsweetened cocoa
½ teaspoon baking powder
¼ teaspoon salt
⅓ cup milk
1 cup **REESE'S® Pieces**

Cream butter, sugar, egg and vanilla until light and fluffy. Combine flour, cocoa, baking powder and salt; add alternately with milk to creamed mixture. Stir in 1 cup peanut butter pieces. Drop by teaspoonsful 2-inches apart onto lightly greased cookie sheet. Bake at 350° for 7 to 9 minutes or until set, but not dry. Cool slightly; remove from cookie sheet onto wire rack.

About 4 dozen cookies

Roman Meal® Spice Drops

½ cup shortening
1½ cups brown sugar, packed
3 eggs, slightly beaten
¼ cup milk
1 tsp. vanilla
1⅔ cups sifted flour
1½ tsp. baking powder
½ tsp. salt
1 tsp. each of cinnamon, nutmeg and cloves
2 cups **ROMAN MEAL® Cereal**
1 cup raisins
1 cup chopped nuts (optional)

Cream shortening and sugar. Blend in eggs, milk and vanilla. Add flour sifted with baking powder, spices and salt; mix thoroughly. Add cereal, raisins and nuts. Drop from teaspoon about 2 inches apart onto cookie sheet. Bake 10-12 minutes at 375°F.

Makes 4-5 dozen cookies

"Lady Be Good" Fingers

1 teaspoon soft butter
½ teaspoon grated orange or lemon rind
½ cup **DOMINO® Confectioners 10-X Powdered Sugar**
2 teaspoons orange or lemon juice
1 dozen lady fingers, split

Blend butter and rind. Alternately add sugar and juice, mixing until smooth. Spread a thin layer of fruit glaze between lady fingers. Sprinkle with more sugar. Serve at once, or store in air tight container.

Kellogg's
Marshmallow Treats

¼ cup margarine or butter
1 package (10 oz., about 40) regular marshmallows or 4
   cups miniature marshmallows
5 cups **KELLOGG'S® RICE KRISPIES® Cereal**

Melt margarine in large saucepan over low heat. Add marshmallows and stir until completely melted. Cook over low heat 3 minutes longer, stirring constantly. Remove from heat. Add cereal. Stir until well coated. Using buttered spatula or waxed paper, press mixture evenly into buttered 13 × 9 × 2-inch pan. Cut into 2-inch squares when cool.

Yield: 24 squares, 2 × 2 inches

Note: Best results are obtained when using fresh marshmallows.

VARIATIONS:

To make thicker squares: Press warm mixture into buttered 9 × 9 × 2-inch pan.

Marshmallow Creme Treats

About 2 cups marshmallow creme may be substituted for marshmallows. Add to melted margarine and stir until well blended. Cook over low heat about 5 minutes longer, stirring constantly. Remove from heat. Proceed as directed above.

Peanut Treats

Add 1 cup salted cocktail peanuts with the cereal.

Peanut Butter Treats

Stir ¼ cup peanut butter into marshmallow mixture just before adding the cereal.

Raisin Treats

Add 1 cup seedless raisins with the cereal.

Cocoa Krispies® Cereal Treats

6 cups **KELLOGG'S® COCOA KRISPIES® Cereal** may be substituted for the 5 cups **KELLOGG'S® RICE KRISPIES® Cereal**.

® Kellogg Company

ARGO®/KINGSFORD'S®
Chinese Almond Cookies

2¼ cups unsifted flour
½ cup **ARGO®/KINGSFORD'S® Corn Starch**
1 teaspoon baking powder
¼ teaspoon salt
1 egg
¾ cup sugar
¼ cup **KARO® Light Corn Syrup**
⅔ cup **MAZOLA® Corn Oil**
2 teaspoons almond extract
1 teaspoon vanilla extract
⅓ cup whole blanched almonds

In small bowl stir together flour, corn starch, baking powder and salt. In large bowl with mixer at medium speed beat egg until frothy. Gradually add sugar and corn syrup; beat until thoroughly mixed. In small bowl stir together corn oil and extracts. Gradually add to egg mixture, beating until well mixed. Add flour mixture in 2 additions, beating until smooth. Shape into 1-inch balls. Place about 2½ inches apart on greased cookie sheet. Flatten with lightly floured bottom of glass to ⅛-inch thickness. Place almond in center of each. Bake in 350°F oven 10 to 12 minutes or until lightly browned. Remove to wire rack. Cool completely. Store in tightly covered container. *Makes about 4 dozen*

Libby's
Libby's
Libby's
Fireside Pumpkin Cookies

1 cup butter or margarine
½ cup light brown sugar, firmly packed
½ cup granulated sugar
1 cup **LIBBY'S® Solid Pack Pumpkin**
1 egg
1 teaspoon vanilla
2 cups sifted flour
1 teaspoon baking soda
1 teaspoon baking powder
1 teaspoon ground cinnamon
½ teaspoon salt
1 cup chopped walnuts
1 cup snipped dates

Preheat oven to 350°F. In a large bowl, beat butter and sugars together until fluffy. Add pumpkin, egg and vanilla; mix well. Sift flour, baking soda, baking powder, cinnamon and salt together. Add to pumpkin mixture and stir to mix well. Stir in nuts and dates. Drop batter by heaping teaspoonfuls onto ungreased baking sheets, 1 inch apart. Bake at 350° for 15 minutes or until tops are golden and centers firm to the touch. Remove from baking sheets and cool on wire racks. *Yields about 4 dozen 2-inch cookies*

Elam's
Wheat Germ Sour Cream Cookies

2 cups **ELAM'S® Unbleached White Flour with
   Wheat Germ**
1 teaspoon baking soda
½ teaspoon salt
¾ teaspoon nutmeg
1 cup **ELAM'S® Natural Wheat Germ**
¾ cup butter
1½ cups (packed) brown sugar
2 teaspoons vanilla
1 teaspoon finely shredded lemon rind
2 eggs
½ cup thick sour cream
½ cup chopped pecans or walnuts

Combine and sift first 4 ingredients into bowl. Stir in wheat germ; reserve. Beat butter until creamy. Add brown sugar, vanilla and lemon rind; beat until fluffy. Add eggs, one at a time; beat well after each addition. Add dry ingredients and sour cream alternately to creamed mixture; blend well after each addition. Stir in chopped nuts. Drop rounded tablespoonfuls of dough onto lightly greased baking sheets. Bake in moderate oven (350°F.) until done and lightly browned, 12 to 14 minutes.

Yield: 4 dozen cookies, about 2½ inches in diameter

No-Bake Cookies

¼ cup butter or margarine
⅓ cup peanut butter
¼ cup maple flavored syrup
2 tablespoons firmly packed brown sugar
3 cups coarsely crushed **QUAKER® 100% Natural Cereal**, original (about 3½ cups cereal)

Combine all ingredients except cereal in 1-qt. saucepan; bring to a boil. Simmer over medium heat about 3 minutes, stirring constantly. Pour over cereal; mix well. Press into greased 8-inch square baking pan. Chill until firm; cut into bars. Store in refrigerator. *Makes 8-inch square pan of no-bake cookies*

Brown Sugar Drop Cookies

1 egg
1 cup brown sugar, firmly packed
1 tsp. vanilla
½ cup unsifted all-purpose flour
¼ tsp. soda
¼ tsp. salt
1½ cups **DIAMOND® Walnuts**, chopped medium fine

In small mixer bowl beat egg till it is light and fluffy (about 3 min. at high speed). Add sugar and vanilla and stir till smooth. Quickly stir in flour, soda and salt. Blend in walnuts chopped medium fine. By teaspoonfuls, drop onto greased and floured cookie sheet 2 inches apart. Bake at 350°F., 7-9 min. Or just till cookies start to brown at edge. Do not overbake. Remove immediately to cooling rack. *Makes about 4 dozen 2-inch cookies*

Butterscotch Crispies

1½ cups sifted flour
¼ teaspoon salt
1¼ teaspoons baking powder
½ cup butter or shortening
⅔ cup brown sugar
1 teaspoon vanilla
1 egg
¾ cup crushed **JAYS Potato Chips**

Sift flour once, then measure; add salt and baking powder and sift together three times. Cream shortening and sugar together until light and fluffy. Add vanilla and egg and beat well. Gradually add flour, mixing well after addition. Add potato chips. Shape in a two-inch roll and wrap in wax paper. Chill overnight in refrig-

erator. Cut in ⅛ inch slices. Bake on ungreased cooky sheet in moderately hot 375 degree oven for 10 to 12 minutes or until lightly browned. Keep cookies in tightly covered can or jar.

Makes 4 dozen

Lemon Thins

½ lb. (2 sticks) **DARIGOLD Butter**
1 cup white sugar
1 **DARIGOLD Egg**
1¾ cups flour
¼ teaspoon salt
Juice and rind of 1 lemon

Cream **DARIGOLD Butter** and sugar. Add egg, flour, salt and lemon. Roll into a roll 2″ thick and 12″ long. Place in refrigerator to chill. Slice thin and bake in 375 degree oven on greased cookie sheets 8 to 10 minutes or until edges turn light brown.

Libby's
Libby's
Libby's

Pumpkin Dandies

1 cup **LIBBY'S® Solid Pack Pumpkin**
1 cup sugar
1¼ cups flaked coconut, lightly packed
½ teaspoon ground cinnamon
¼ teaspoon ground nutmeg
Finely chopped walnuts or peanuts
Red and green candied cherries, optional

In a large heavy saucepan, combine pumpkin, sugar, coconut and spices; mix well. Cook over medium-high heat, stirring constantly, for about 15 to 20 minutes. Candy is done when it becomes very thick and leaves the side of pan, forming a ball in center as you stir. Turn mixture out onto a buttered baking sheet; cover loosely with foil or plastic wrap; let cool completely. Lightly butter hands and shape candy into balls; roll in chopped nuts. Top each with a candied cherry half if desired. Cover and store in refrigerator. *Yields about 2½ dozen candies*

VARIATION:

For a crunchier candy, stir 1 cup crushed 100% natural cereal into cooked candy before cooling and shaping.

Santa's Whiskers

1 cup butter or margarine
1 cup sugar
1 teaspoon **DURKEE Almond Extract**
2½ cups all purpose flour
¾ cup finely chopped **DURKEE Maraschino Cherries** (1 10 oz. jar)
½ cup finely chopped pecans
¾ cup **DURKEE Flaked Coconut**

Cream butter and sugar, blend in extract. Stir in flour, cherries, and nuts. Form in 2 rolls, each 2 inches in diameter and 8 inches long. Roll in coconut. Wrap and chill several hours or overnight. Slice ¼ inch thick; place on ungreased cookie sheet. Bake at 375° for 12 minutes or until edges are golden. *Makes about 5 dozen*

Giant Oatmeal Cookies

1¼ cups all-purpose flour
½ teaspoon soda
½ teaspoon salt
1 cup firmly packed brown sugar
¾ cup butter or margarine
2 eggs
1 teaspoon vanilla
2½ cups **QUAKER® Oats** (quick or old fashioned, uncooked)
One 6-oz. pkg. (1 cup) semi-sweet chocolate pieces
½ cup chopped nuts

Heat oven to 350°F. Grease 2 large cookie sheets. In small bowl, combine flour, soda and salt; mix well. In large bowl, beat together sugar and butter until light and fluffy; blend in eggs and vanilla. Add flour mixture; mix well. Stir in oats, chocolate pieces and nuts. Divide dough in half. Spread each half to ¾-inch thickness on prepared cookie sheets. Bake 17 to 20 minutes or until lightly browned. Decorate with candles, if desired.

Makes two 11-inch cookies

VARIATION:

Drop dough by rounded tablespoonfuls onto greased cookie sheets. Bake 10 to 12 minutes.

Makes about 3 dozen 2½-inch cookies

Peanut Butter Crunchies

1 cup (2 sticks) **MEADOW GOLD® Butter**
1 cup granulated sugar
1 cup packed dark brown sugar
1 cup chunky peanut butter
2 eggs
1 teaspoon vanilla
2¾ cups sifted all-purpose flour
½ teaspoon soda
⅛ teaspoon salt
Granulated sugar

Beat butter, sugars and peanut butter until light and fluffy. Beat in eggs and vanilla. Sift together dry ingredients. Add gradually to butter mixture, mixing well. Shape into 1-inch balls. Dip half of ball into sugar; place on ungreased cookie sheet with sugar-side up. Flatten with fork. Bake at 350° for 10 minutes or until lightly browned.
8 dozen

Sachertorte Cookies

1 cup margarine or butter, softened
4½ oz. pkg. instant chocolate pudding and pie filling mix
1 egg
2 cups **PILLSBURY'S BEST® All Purpose Flour**
3 tablespoons sugar
½ cup apricot or cherry preserves
½ cup semi-sweet chocolate chips
3 tablespoons margarine or butter, melted

Heat oven to 325°F. In large bowl, cream margarine and pudding mix until light and fluffy; beat in egg. Lightly spoon flour into measuring cup; level off. Gradually add flour at low speed until well mixed and dough forms. Shape into 1-inch balls, roll in sugar. Place 2 inches apart on ungreased cookie sheets. With thumb, make imprint in center of each cookie. Bake at 325°F. for 15 to 18 minutes or until firm to touch. Remove from cookie sheets immediately. Cool. Fill each imprint with ½ teaspoon preserves. In small saucepan, blend chocolate chips and margarine over low heat until chocolate melts, stirring constantly. Drizzle ½ teaspoon over each cookie.
48 cookies

HIGH ALTITUDE—Above 3500 Feet: Bake at 350°F. for 12 to 15 minutes.

Peanut Butter & Jelly Thumbprints

1 cup butter or margarine, softened
1¾ cups packed brown sugar
2 eggs
2 teaspoons vanilla
3 cups unsifted all-purpose flour
1 teaspoon baking powder
1 teaspoon salt
1½ cups quick-cooking oatmeal
2 cups (12-ounce package) **REESE'S® Peanut Butter Flavored Chips**
¾ cup jelly or preserves (apple, grape, peach, etc.)

Cream butter or margarine and brown sugar in large mixer bowl. Add eggs and vanilla; beat until light and fluffy. Combine flour, baking powder and salt in small bowl; add to creamed mixture. Reserve ½ cup peanut butter chips; stir in oatmeal and 1½ cups peanut butter chips. Shape small amounts of dough into 1-inch balls. Place balls on ungreased cookie sheet; press with thumb into center making deep depression about 1-inch wide. Bake at 400°F. for 7 to 9 minutes or until lightly browned. Remove from cookie sheet; cool on wire rack. Fill center of each cookie with ½ teaspoon jelly or preserves; top with several peanut butter chips.

About 5 dozen 2½-inch cookies

Candies

IMPERIAL Pure Cane SUGAR.

Cane-Fest Pralines

2 cups **IMPERIAL Granulated Sugar**
1 teaspoon soda
1 cup buttermilk
⅛ teaspoon salt
2 tablespoons butter or margarine
2½ cups pecan halves

In large (3½ quart) heavy saucepan combine **IMPERIAL Granulated Sugar**, soda, buttermilk and salt. Cook over high heat about 5 minutes (or to 210°F. on candy thermometer); stir often and scrape bottom of pan. Mixture will foam up. Add butter or margarine and pecans. Over medium heat, continue cooking, stirring constantly and scraping bottom and sides of pan until candy reaches soft ball stage (234°F. on candy thermometer). Remove from heat and cool slightly, about 2 minutes. Beat with spoon until thick and creamy. Drop from tablespoon onto sheet of aluminum foil or waxed paper. Let cool.

Makes about 20 pralines, 2" in diameter

Five-Minute Fudge

2 tablespoons butter
⅔ cup undiluted **CARNATION® Evaporated Milk**
1⅔ cups sugar
½ teaspoon salt
2 cups (4 ounces) miniature marshmallows
1½ cups (1½ 6-ounce packages) semi-sweet chocolate pieces
1 teaspoon vanilla
½ cup chopped nuts

Combine butter, evaporated milk, sugar, and salt in saucepan over medium heat, stirring occasionally. Bring to full boil. Cook 4 to 5 minutes, stirring constantly. Remove from heat. Stir in marshmallows, chocolate pieces, vanilla, and nuts. Stir vigorously for 1 minute (until marshmallows melt and blend). Pour into 8-inch square buttered pan. Cool. Cut in squares. *Makes 2 pounds*

Nestlé
Creamy Chocolate Fudge

1 jar marshmallow cream*
1½ cups sugar
⅔ cup evaporated milk
¼ cup butter
¼ measuring teaspoon salt
One 11½ oz. pkg. (2 cups) **NESTLÉ Milk Chocolate Morsels**
One 6-oz. pkg. (1 cup) **NESTLÉ Semi-Sweet Real Chocolate Morsels**
½ cup chopped nuts
1 measuring teaspoon vanilla extract

In large saucepan, combine marshmallow cream, sugar, evaporated milk, butter and salt; bring to *full boil* over moderate heat, stirring constantly. *Boil 5 minutes*, stirring constantly over moderate heat. Remove from heat. Add **NESTLÉ Milk Chocolate Morsels and NESTLÉ Semi-Sweet Real Chocolate Morsels**; stir until morsels melt and mixture is well blended. Stir in nuts and vanilla extract. Pour into aluminum foil-lined 8" square pan. Chill in refrigerator until firm (about 2 hours).
5 oz.—10 oz. jar *Makes: 2½ lbs. candy*

Chocolate Almond Bark

One 11½-oz. pkg. (2 cups) **NESTLÉ Milk Chocolate Morsels**
1 measuring tablespoon vegetable shortening
½ cup raisins
½ cup chopped toasted almonds, divided

Combine over hot (not boiling) water, **NESTLÉ Milk Chocolate Morsels** and vegetable shortening. Heat until morsels are melted and mixture is smooth. Remove from heat and stir in raisins and half the almonds. Spread into waxed paper-lined 13″ × 9″ × 2″ baking pan*. Sprinkle remaining almonds on top. Chill in refrigerator until ready to serve, at least 30 minutes. Before serving, break into bite-size pieces. *Makes 1-lb. candy*

*Make waxed paper long enough so that candy can be easily lifted out of the pan.

MICROWAVE METHOD:
To melt, in a 4-cup glass measuring cup, add **NESTLÉ Milk Chocolate Morsels**. Microwave on high 2 minutes; stir. Microwave on high 1 minute longer. Stir until chocolate is smooth.
Makes: 1 cup melted chocolate

Fantasy Fudge

3 cups sugar
¾ cup **PARKAY Margarine**
⅔ cup (5⅓-fl. oz. can) evaporated milk
1 12-oz. pkg. semi-sweet chocolate pieces
1 7-oz. jar **KRAFT Marshmallow Creme**
1 cup chopped nuts
1 teaspoon vanilla

Combine sugar, margarine and milk in heavy saucepan; bring to full rolling boil, stirring constantly. Continue boiling 5 minutes over medium heat, stirring constantly to prevent scorching. Remove from heat; stir in chocolate until melted. Add marshmallow creme, nuts and vanilla; beat until well blended. Pour into greased 13 × 9-inch baking pan. Cool at room temperature; cut into squares. *3 pounds*

EAGLE®BRAND
Foolproof Chocolate Fudge

3 (6-ounce) packages semi-sweet chocolate morsels
1 (14-ounce) can **EAGLE® Brand Sweetened Condensed Milk** (NOT evaporated milk)
Dash salt
1½ teaspoons vanilla extract
½ cup chopped nuts, optional

In heavy saucepan, over low heat, melt morsels with **EAGLE® Brand**. Remove from heat; stir in remaining ingredients. Spread evenly into wax paper-lined 8-inch square pan. Chill 2 to 3 hours or until firm. Turn fudge onto cutting board; peel off paper and cut into squares. Store loosely covered at room temperature.
Makes about 1¾ pounds

VARIATION:

Rocky Road Fudge

Omit 1 (6-ounce) package semi-sweet chocolate morsels, salt, vanilla and nuts. In saucepan, melt morsels with **EAGLE® Brand** and 2 tablespoons margarine. In large bowl, combine 2 cups dry roasted peanuts and 1 (10½-ounce) package miniature marshmallows. Pour chocolate mixture into nut mixture; mix well. Spread into wax paper-lined 13x9-inch pan. Chill 2 hours.

Acknowledgments

The Editors of CONSUMER GUIDE® wish to thank the companies and organizations listed for use of their recipes and artwork. For further information contact the following:

Alba, *see* Heinz U.S.A.

Almadén Vineyards
San Jose, CA 95150

Amaretto di Galliano™, *see* "21" Brands

American Beauty®, *see* Pillsbury Co.

American Egg Board
1460 Renaissance
Park Ridge, IL 60068

Angostura®—A-W Brands, Inc.
Carteret, NJ 07008

Argo®/Kingsford's®, *see* Best Foods

Arrow®—Heublein/Spirits Group
330 New Park Ave.
Hartford, CT 06101

Azteca Corn Products Corp.
4850 S. Austin
Chicago, IL 60638-1491

Baker's®, *see* General Foods

Banquet Foods Corp.
Ballwin, MO 63011

Batter-Lite®—Batterlite Whitlock Inc.
P.O. Box 259
Springfield, IL 62705

Bays English Muffin Corp.
500 N. Michigan Ave.
Chicago, IL 60611

Bénédictine, *see* Wile, Julius, Sons & Co., Inc.

Bertolli U.S.A.
P.O. Box 931
So. San Francisco, CA 94080

Best Foods
Englewood Cliffs, NJ 07632

Betty Crocker®, *see* General Mills, Inc.

Birds Eye® Cool Whip®, *see* General Foods

Bisquick®, *see* General Mills, Inc.

Blue Diamond®—Calif. Almond Growers Exch.
P.O. Box 1768
Sacramento, CA 95808

Blue Ribbon®—Continental Nut Co.
Chico, CA 95927

Borden Inc.
180 E. Broad St.
Columbus, OH 43215

Bordo Products Co.
2825 Sheffield Ave.
Chicago, IL 60657

Bran Chex®, *see* Ralston Purina Co.

Breakstone's®, *see* Kraft Inc.—Dairy Group

Breyers®, *see* Kraft, Inc.—Dairy Group

Butter Buds®, *see* Cumberland Packing

Calavo Growers of California
Box 3486 Terminal Annex
Los Angeles, CA 90051

California Brandy Advisory Board
426 Pacific Ave.
San Francisco, CA 94133

Calumet®, *see* General Foods

Campbell Soup Co.
Camden, NJ 08101

Canada Dry Corp.
100 Park Ave.
New York, NY 10017

Cape Granny Smith Apples
Dudley, Anderson, Yutzy
40 W. 57th St.
New York, NY 10019

Carnation
5045 Wilshire Blvd.
Los Angeles, CA 90036

Ceresota, *see* Standard Milling Co.

Chiquita Brands, Inc.
Montvale, NJ 07645

Christian Brothers®, *The*—Fromm and Sichel, Inc.
San Francisco, CA 94120

Clark Co., D. L.
503 Martindale St.
Pittsburgh, PA 15212

Coca-Cola Co., The
P.O. Drawer 1734
Atlanta, GA 30301

Coco Casa™, *see* Holland House Brands Co.

CocoRibe®—National Distillers and Chemical Corp.
99 Park Ave.
New York, NY 10016

Colonial Sugars, Inc.
Mobile, AL 36633

Continental, *see* Globe Products Co., Inc.

Courvoisier®, *see* Taylor, W.A., & Co.

Cracker Barrel, *see* Kraft, Inc.

Crisco®, *see* Procter & Gamble Co.

Cumberland Packing Corp.
Brooklyn, NY 11205

Dannon Co., The.
22-11 38th Ave.
Long Island, NY 11101

Darigold—Consolidated Dairy Products Co.
635 Elliott Ave. W.
Seattle, WA 98109

Del Monte Corp.
P.O. Box 3575
San Francisco, CA 94119

Dia-Mel, *see* Estee Corp., The

Diamond®, *see* Sun-Diamond

Diet Shasta®—Shasta Beverages
Hayward, CA 94545

Dole®—Castle & Cooke Foods
50 California St.
San Francisco, CA 94119

Domino®—Amstar Corp.
1251 Avenue of the Americas
New York, NY 10020

Dorman, N., & Co.
Syosset, NY 11791

Drambuie®, *see* Taylor, W. A., & Co.

Dream Whip®, *see* General Foods

Dromedary, *see* Nabisco Brands Inc.

Droste®, *see* Wile, Julius, Sons & Co.

Dry Sack®, *see* Wile, Julius, Sons & Co.

Dubonnet, *see* Schenley Affiliated Brands Corp.

DuBouchett, *see* Schenley Affiliated Brands Corp.

Duncan Hines®, *see* Procter & Gamble Co.

Durkee Foods—Div. of SCM Corp.
Strongsville, OH 44136

E-Z-Bake—Acme Evans Co.
902 W. Washington Ave.
Indianapolis, IN 46204

Eagle® Brand, *see* Borden Inc.

Elam Mills
Broadview, IL 60153

Estee Corp., The
Parsippany, NJ 07054

Featherweight®—Chicago Dietetic Supply, Inc.
La Grange, IL 60525

Fireside—Doumak Illinois, Inc.
2491 Estes Ave.
Elk Grove Village, IL 60007

Fisher Nut Co.
St. Paul, MN 55164

Fleischmann's®, *see* Nabisco Brands, Inc.

Frangelico®—Wm. Grant & Sons, Inc.
Edison, NJ 08817

French, R.T., Co.
Rochester, NY 14609

Friendly
Wilbraham, MA 01095

Frostlite™, *see* Batterlite Whitlock, Inc.

General Foods Corp.
White Plains, NY 10625

General Mills, Inc.
Minneapolis, MN 55440

Gerber Products Co.
Fremont, MI 49412

Ghiradelli®—Golden Grain Macaroni Co.
San Leandro, CA 94578

Giroux®—Iroquois Grocery Products
111 High Ridge Rd.
Stamford, CT 06902

Globe Products Co., Inc.
Clifton, NJ 07015

Gold Medal®, *see* General Mills, Inc.

Guittard Chocolate Co.
Burlingame, CA 94010

Health Valley Natural Foods
700 Union St.
Montebello, CA 90640

Heartland®, *see* Pet

Heath, L. S. & Sons, Inc.
Robinson, IL 62454

Hecker's, *see* Standard Milling Co.

Heinz U.S.A.
Pittsburgh, PA 15212

Hellmann's®, *see* Best Foods

Hershey Foods Corp.
Hershey, PA 17033

Hiram Walker Inc.
P.O. Box 33006
Detroit, MI 48232

Holland House Brands Co.
Ridgefield, NJ 07657

Honey Maid, *see* Nabisco Brands, Inc.

Hungry Jack®, *see* Pillsbury Co., The

Hydrox®, *see* Sunshine Biscuits, Inc.

Imperial Sugar Company
P.O. Box 50129
Dallas, TX 75250

International Multifoods
Eighth & Marquette
Minneapolis, MN 55402

Iroquois Grocery Products, Inc.
111 High Ridge Rd.
Stamford, CT 06902

Jays Foods, Inc.
825 E. 99th St.
Chicago, IL 60628

Jell-O® Brand, *see* General Foods

Jif®, *see* Procter & Gamble Co.

Jiffy®, *see* Borden Inc.

Johnnie Walker Red, *see* Somerset Importers

Kahlúa®—Maidstone Wine & Spirits, Inc.
70 Universal City Plaza
Universal City, CA 91608

Karo®, *see* Best Foods

Keebler Co.
Elmhurst, IL 60126

Kellogg Company
Battle Creek, MI 49016

Kingsford's®, *see* Best Foods

Kitchen Bouquet®—The Clorox Co.
Oakland, CA 94623

Knox®—Thomas J. Lipton, Inc.
Englewood Cliffs, NJ 07632

Kraft, Inc.
Glenview, IL 60025

Kraft, Inc.—Dairy Group
P.O. Box 7830
Philadelphia, PA 19101

Kretschmer, *see* International Multifoods

La Choy Food Products
Archbold, OH 43502

Laird's, *see* Taylor, W. A., & Co.

Land O' Lakes, Inc.
P.O. Box 116
Minneapolis, MN 55440

Lawry Foods, Inc.
570 West Avenue 26
Los Angeles, CA 90065

Lemon Hart, *see* Wile, Julius, & Sons Co., Inc.

Libby, McNeill & Libby, Inc.
200 S. Michigan Ave.
Chicago, IL 60604

Liquore Galliano®, *see* "21" Brands, Inc.

Log Cabin®, *see* General Foods

Louis Sherry Ice Cream Co., Inc.
400 Calvert Ave.
Alexandria, VA 22301

Lucky Leaf®—Knouse Foods Cooperative, Inc.
Peach Glen, PA 17306

M&M/Mars
Hackettstown, NJ 07840

Malt-O-Meal Co.
1520 TCF Towers
Minneapolis, MN 55402

Mandarine Napoléon, *see* Somerset Importers

Marshmallow Fluff®—Durkee-Mower, Inc.
Lynn, MA 01903

Mazola®, *see* Best Foods

Meadow Gold Dairies
1526 S. State St.
Chicago, IL 60605

Medaglia D'Oro®—Schronbrunn, S. A.
Palisades Park, NJ 07650

Metaxa®, *see* Wile, Julius, Sons & Co.

Migliore®—Scheps Cheese
Haledon, NJ 07538

Milk Duds®—D. L. Clark Co. (Branch)
308 W. Ontario St.
Chicago, IL 60610

Milnot Company
Litchfield, IL 62056

Minute®, *see* General Foods

Minute Maid®—The Coca-Cola Co.
P.O. Box 2079
Houston, TX 77001

Mueller Co., C. F.
Jersey City, NJ 07306

Nabisco Brands, Inc.
625 Madison Ave.
New York, NY 10022

Nestlé Company, The
White Plains, NY 10605

New Zealand Kiwifruit Authority
55 Union St.
San Francisco, CA 94111

Nilla, *see* Nabisco Brands, Inc.

None Such®, *see* Borden Inc.

Nucoa®, *see* Best Foods

Oreo, *see* Nabisco Brands, Inc.

Parkay, *see* Kraft, Inc.

Pepperidge Farm, Inc.
Norwalk, CT 06856

Pet
St. Louis, MO 63166

Peter Pan®, *see* Swift & Co.

Philadelphia Brand, *see* Kraft, Inc.

Pillsbury Co., The
Minneapolis, MN 55402

Planters®, *see* Nabisco Brands, Inc.

Post®, *see* General Foods

Praline®, *see* Hiram Walker Inc.

Procter & Gamble Co.
Cincinnati, OH 45202

Puritan®, *see* Procter & Gamble Co.

Quaker Oats Company, The
Chicago, IL 60654

Raffetto®, *see* Iroquois Grocery Products,
Inc.

Ralston Purina Co.
St. Louis, MO 63188

ReaLemon®, *see* Borden Inc.

ReaLime®, *see* Borden Inc.

Red Star®—Universal Foods Corp.
Milwaukee, WI 53201

Reese's®, *see* Hershey Foods Corp.

Robin Hood®, *see* International Multifoods

Rold Gold®—Frito-Lay, Inc.
P.O. Box 35034
Dallas, TX 75235

Roman Meal Company
Tacoma, WA 98411

Roquefort Association, Inc.
41 E. 42nd St.
New York, NY 10017

Royal, *see* Nabisco Brands, Inc.

S&W Fine Foods, Inc.
San Mateo, CA 94402

Sara Lee, Kitchens of
Deerfield, IL 60015

Schenley Affiliated Brands Corp.
888 Seventh Ave.
New York, NY 10106

Sealtest®, *see* Kraft Inc.—Dairy Group

Simon Fischer, *see* Globe Products Co.,
Inc.

Skippy®, *see* Best Foods

Smucker, J. M. Co., The
Orrville, OH 44667

Snack Mate, *see* Nabisco Brands, Inc.

Softasilk®, *see* General Mills, Inc.

Solo®—Sokol and Company
Countryside, IL 60525

Somerset Importers
1114 Avenue of the Americas
New York, NY 10036-7755

Southern Belle, *see* Nabisco Brands, Inc.

Standard Milling Company
1009 Central St.
Kansas City, MO 64141

Stokely-Van Camp, Inc.
Indianapolis, IN 46206

Success®—Rivinia Foods, Inc.
P.O. Box 2636
Houston, TX 77001

Sue Bee®—Sioux Honey Association
Sioux City, IA 51102

Sun World, Inc.
5544 California Ave.
Bakersfield, CA 93309

Sun-Diamond Growers of California
San Ramon, CA 94583

Sunkist Growers, Inc.
Van Nuys, CA 91409

Sunlite®—Hunt-Wesson Kitchens
Fullerton, CA 92634

Sun-Maid®, *see* Sun-Diamond Growers

Sunshine Biscuits, Inc.
245 Park Ave.
New York, NY 10017

Sunsweet®, *see* Sun-Diamond

Swans Down®, *see* General Foods

Sweet 'N Low®, *see* Cumberland Packing
Corp.

Sweetlite™, *see* Batterlite Whitlock Inc.

Swift & Company
Oak Brook, IL 60521

Tang™, *see* General Foods

Taylor, W.A. & Co.
825 S. Bayshore Dr.
Miami, FL 33131

Texas Citrus Advertising, Inc.
P.O. Box 2497
McAllen, TX 78501

Thank You® Brand—Michigan Fruit
Canners
Benton Harbor, MI 49022

3-Minute Brand®—National Oats Co. Inc.
1515 H Ave. NE
Cedar Rapids, IA 52402

Tia Maria®, *see* Taylor, W. A., Co.

Tom's Foods
P.O. Box 60
Columbus, GA 31994

''21'' Brands, Inc.
75 Rockefeller Plaza
New York, NY 10019

Uncle Ben's Foods
P.O. Box 1752
Houston, TX 77001

Virginia Dare Extract Co.
822 Third Ave.
Brooklyn, NY 11232

Weight Watchers®—Foodways National
Inc.
P.O. Box 41
Boise, ID 83707

Welch Foods Inc.
Westfield, NY 14787

Wild Turkey Liqueur®—Austin Nichols &
Co. Inc.
1290 Avenue of the Americas
New York, NY 10104

Wile, Julius, Sons & Co., Inc.
Lake Success, NY 11042

Wolff's®—The Birkett Mills
Penn Yan, NY 14527

Index